A Word For Today

A Year Round
Daily Devotional
And Prayer Journal Book

Tinu Banjo

A Word For Today

Published by Cornerstone Publishing
A Division of Cornerstone Creativity Group LLC
Info@thecornerstonepublishers.com
www.thecornerstonepublishers.com

Author's Contact
To book the author to speak at your next event or to order bulk copies of this book, please, use the information below:
bantfor@gmail.com || https://lekeandtinubanjo.com

Printed in the United States of America.

Dedication

This book is dedicated to the brave frontline workers who cared for the sick during the COVID-19 Pandemic.

To the lives lost, the survivors, and those who continue to stand strong.

To God's sovereignty over mankind in the global lockdown era.

To the incredible creativity of humanity, which birthed various life-transforming gadgets, businesses, and new careers that emerged as a means of survival, joy, and laughter amidst countless losses. You are truly unique.

Preface

The Word for Today Devotional Prayer Journal was birthed on April 1, 2021, after a divine burden to reach out to others during the period of the Covid-19 pandemic lockdown.

Prior to the pandemic, I held a monthly prayer meeting with a women's group, but we were no longer able to meet physically. However, the desire to reach out to the group remained strong, as other social media platforms such as Zoom, Teams, and telephone conference lines were not as effective. I shared this burden with a beloved sister and mentor, who encouraged me to reach out through a minute of prayer based on a Bible text led by the Holy Spirit.

The Lord gave me the revelation for a daily word of prayer from Bible scripture readings as a word for today on a women's platform. That was how I began the journey towards this daily devotional in your hands. It was initially tedious because it is a daily devotional, and there were times when I was very reluctant to continue. However, the grace of God was sufficient every day with the help of the Holy Spirit, who always nudged and reminded me of the Rhema of His word when I did not have content for the next day's post.

To the glory and grace of God, I was able to complete the

devotional and received a lot of encouragement and nudging to publish it in order to bless others and many people hungry to receive a word from God each morning before they start their day. Many past recipients have admitted to reposting it on other social media platforms for their families and friends to partake in the devotional.

As you take the step of faith to read each Bible verse, encouraging words, and confess heartfelt prayers, my prayer is that this devotional will bless and fill you with the assurance of God's love every day. I pray that it will give you the confidence to step out boldly each day, knowing that the presence of God is with you throughout the day. I pray that the Word for Today Daily Devotional strengthens your intimate relationship with the Lord Jesus Christ through His word. I pray that this devotional reminds you of who you are in the Lord Jesus Christ as you start your day and empowers you to achieve all that God has in store for you daily. In Jesus' name, amen.

Love and blessings,

Tinu Banjo

ACKNOWLEDGMENTS

I am grateful to the King of kings and the Lord of lords for His daily watchful care over me. It's overwhelming to realize how deeply loved I am by a Father who sacrificed His life for me, even when I was lost in sin. Lord Jesus, not only did you cleanse me, but you also entrusted me with the task, opening my mind to receive the divine message in this book. Thank you for paying the ultimate price for my redemption. I cherish this gift and strive to bring you joy every day.

I want to express my deepest gratitude to my amazing husband for your constant love, unwavering encouragement, and for nurturing greatness within me. You've provided platforms for me to showcase the rich deposits of God's gifts. Sweetheart, you are not just a blessing to me but to this entire generation; I love and cherish you immensely.

To my dear children, Tokunbo, Jasmine, Temi, Toyin, Tosin, and Timmy, you have been my greatest supporters and cheerleaders in every endeavor. As part of our "BE AMAZING, NEVER JUST ORDINARY CLAN," you continuously inspire and motivate me to strive for excellence and pursue my dreams relentlessly. I pray that your own children will also rise up and call you blessed, just as you bless me daily.

I want to extend heartfelt thanks to all my spiritual mentors who have generously invested their time to impart the life-giving Word of God into me through their exemplary lives of mentorship. Your actions speak louder than words, and I am deeply grateful.

To my church family at RCCG worldwide, most especially my beloved New Wine Family, from the youngest to the oldest, thank you for embracing me despite my overwhelming display of love. Your reciprocity means the world to me.

I also want to express my profound appreciation to my esteemed publisher. Your dedication in reviewing, guiding, correcting, and going above and beyond to ensure this book reflects my vision is truly remarkable. It's a blessing to humanity for generations present and future, and I am forever thankful.

Sincerely,

Tinu Banjo

Day 1

*"**And God blessed them**, and God said unto them, be fruitful, and multiply, and replenish the earth, and subdue it: and have dominion over the fish of the sea, and over the fowl of the air, and over every living thing that moveth upon the earth" (Genesis 1:28).*

The blessings for my today are already available to me, as confirmed by God's word in the scriptures above. They are mine for the taking because the word has gone forth; it is settled, and it is established.

———————————————

I will enjoy all the blessings for this season and more today, in Jesus' Name, AMEN.

Personal Prayers Journal

....

....

....

....

....

....

....

Day 2

*"And the angel said unto her, **Fear not**, Mary: for thou hast found favor with God" (Luke 1:30).*

Fear paralyzes, but faith propels. Fear is a limitation to attainment; it limits my focus to the false evidence around me and not on actualizing the goal ahead of me. I choose to face my fear through the power of Christ at work in me.

The propelling faith to accomplish, to break forth, and bring forth all I am destined to achieve is released to me today, in Jesus' Name, AMEN.

Personal Prayers Journal

....

....

....

....

....

....

....

....

....

Day 3

"And the angel said unto them, Fear not: for, behold, I bring you good tidings of great joy, which shall be to all people"
(Luke 2:10).

News of goodness and joy brings gladness to the heart. The good news is a testament to God's goodness and faithfulness in my life. It assures me of His love as He showcases me to the world.

_____

I will only receive news of goodness and joy today. My heart will be filled with joy, and I will speak words of praise throughout the day, in Jesus' name, AMEN.

Personal Prayers Journal

....

....

....

....

....

....

....

....

Day 4

"We walk by Faith and not by Sight" (2 Corinthians 5:7).

Walking by faith means that I am not swayed by what I see, but rather connected to God, who brings about reality and speaks things into existence even when they do not currently exist, all for a purpose.

_____

May all of my plans and purposes become my reality as I take a step of faith today. In Jesus' name, AMEN.

Personal Prayers Journal Journal

....

....

....

....

....

....

....

....

....

....

Day 5

*"I am crucified with Christ: nevertheless, I live; yet not I, but
Christ liveth in me: and the life which I now live in the flesh
I live by the faith of the Son of God, who loved me, and gave
himself for me" (Galatians 2:20).*

A child of God has been ransomed and redeemed through the
crucifixion, death, and resurrection of Jesus. The evidence of
the new birth in Jesus Christ is seen in my transformation by
faith and His abiding presence in me daily.

I declare that I am no longer under condemnation. My life
now has meaning and purpose. I receive strength and courage.
I resist negative pronouncements as I strive to achieve my
goals today, in Jesus' Name.AMEN.

Personal Prayers Journal Journal

....

....

....

....

....

....

Day 6

*"**Blessed is the man that walketh** not in the counsel of the ungodly, nor standeth in the way of sinners, Nor sitteth in the seat of the scornful" (Psalms 1:1).*

Walking involves taking steps in a specific direction. However, taking the wrong step or going in the wrong direction can result in pain, difficulty, or even destruction. Thankfully, with God's presence, I am able to choose the right path towards holiness, righteousness, and daily blessings.

As I embark on this day, I pray for divine speed and guidance. I refuse to remain stagnant, but instead, I will keep moving forward towards my divine blessings and destiny. In Jesus' name, I declare that I will not make the wrong choices that lead to trouble, pain, or death. AMEN.

Personal Prayers Journal Journal

....

....

....

....

....

....

Day 7

*"They shall come with weeping, and with supplications will I lead them: **I will cause them to walk by the rivers of waters** in a straight way, wherein they shall not stumble: for I am a father to Israel, and Ephraim is my firstborn"* (Jeremiah 31:9).

A river of water is a place of refreshing and a source of life with unending resources. The Lord will guide my feet to the place of refreshing and lead me on the straight path.

I will be strategically positioned and refreshed daily. I will walk into abundant resources and be spiritually connected to the life-sustaining power of Jesus as I step out today, in Jesus' Name, AMEN.

Personal Prayers Journal

....

....

....

....

....

....

....

Day 8

"Enter into his gates with thanksgiving, And into his courts with praise: Be thankful unto him, and bless his name"
(Psalms 100:4).

A partnership with God grants me unlimited access into His presence. This door to my divine connection is open as I enter with a heart full of praise and thanksgiving.

———————————

May my heart be always filled with joy and gladness as I step into and connect to His divine presence throughout today, in Jesus Name, AMEN.

Personal Prayers Journal

....

....

....

....

....

....

....

....

Day 9

"And he shall be like a tree planted by the rivers of water, That bringeth forth his fruit in his season; His leaf also shall not wither; And whatsoever he doeth shall prosper" (Psalmss.1:3).

Rivers of water are unending, refreshing, and ever-flowing. My strategic position and location connect me with God, the source of living waters. My relationship with God assures fruitfulness, prosperity, overwhelming joy, and peace.

May my spirit, soul, and body be renewed, refreshed, and rejuvenated to enjoy the unending resources available today, in Jesus' Name, AMEN.

Personal Prayers Journal

....

....

....

....

....

....

....

....

Day 10

*"Thou wilt shew me the path of life: in
thy presence is fulness of joy; at thy right hand there
are pleasures for evermore" (Psalms 16:11).*

God is the one who orders my steps, aligns my path, and
directs my way daily. His right hand, which brings me joy,
guides and leads me every day. He is the only one capable of
showing me the right direction to go because He created the
path I walk on daily.

May the Lord open my eyes to understand as He guides my
path towards my breakthrough and blessings today, in Jesus'
Name. AMEN.

Personal Prayers Journal

....

....

....

....

....

....

....

Day 11

"And as Jesus passed by, he saw a man which was blind from his birth" (John 9:1).

There is divine timing and visitation for a divine miracle. My ability to see Jesus as He passes by me opens the door to my breakthrough. Access to Christ allows Him to do the impossible in my life.

I will receive divine visitation, attention, and answers to all outstanding lifelong issues today, in Jesus' Name. AMEN.

Personal Prayers Journal

....

....

....

....

....

....

....

....

....

....

Day 12

"The fear of the Lord is the beginning of wisdom"
(Psalms 111:10).

Godly reverence draws me closer to the Lord and offers a complete reward for those who walk with Him. As I continue to walk with God, His grace and wisdom fill me more and more, guiding me to discern right from wrong and deepening my reverence for Him.

May my daily walk be characterized by the ability to distinguish between right and wrong, and may I make positive, life-transforming decisions as I connect with Jesus today. In Jesus' Name, AMEN.

Personal Prayers Journal

....

....

....

....

....

....

....

Day 13

*"**How God anointed Jesus of Nazareth with the Holy Ghost and with power,** and he went about doing good, and healing all that were oppressed of the devil for God was with him" (Acts 10:38).*

God's anointing has the power to elevate a person from ordinary to extraordinary. His anointing and the presence of His power in my life enable me to surpass my peers and become a formidable force against the enemy.

May the oil of His anointing and the power of Christ reposition and propel me towards my supernatural greatness today, in Jesus' Name. AMEN

Personal Prayers Journal

....

....

....

....

....

....

....

Day 14

*"How God anointed Jesus of Nazareth with the Holy Ghost and with power, and **he went about doing good**, and healing all that were oppressed of the devil for God was with him"*
(Acts 10:38).

Anointing is the act of consecrating oneself to a life of divine favor and advancement. My personal connection with the Lord Jesus is truly transformative, as it enables me to live a life of complete devotion and serve as a tangible embodiment of His love for others.

———————————————

As I embark on this day, I pray for a divine encounter with the Lord. May I be filled with the boundless love of God, which has the power to bring an end to all forms of illness and oppression, replacing them with undeniable testimonies of miraculous healing, in the name of Jesus. AMEN.

Personal Prayers Journal

....

....

....

....

....

Day 15

*"How God anointed Jesus of Nazareth with the Holy Ghost and with power, and he went about doing good, and healing all that were oppressed of the devil **for God was with him**"* (Acts 10:38).

The presence of God was with Jesus throughout His time on earth, which caused people to be drawn to Him. The evidence of God's presence with me attracts people to gather around me and show me favor every day.

May the presence of God be clearly visible in my life, home, and with my loved ones today and always, in Jesus' Name. AMEN.

Personal Prayers Journal

....

....

....

....

....

....

....

Day 16

*"Samuel said, here is what was kept back. **It was set apart for you. Eat, for it has been kept for you for this occasion"*** (1 Samuel 9:24).

Just like Saul, who was hungry, even though he had a well-prepared meal reserved for him, God knows all of my needs even before I say a word. God is able to provide and meet all of my needs according to His endless riches and unwavering love for me.

May I have access to all of the blessings explicitly reserved for me today. May my spiritual and physical eyes be opened to everything that is rightfully mine to possess today, in Jesus' Name.AMEN.

Personal Prayers Journal

....

....

....

....

....

....

Day 17

"Behold, his soul which is lifted up is not upright in him: but ***the just shall live by his faith"*** *(Habakkuk 2:4).*

Faith is a lifeline for all of God's children. My faith is the key to opening the door to my requests to God. The more I exercise my faith, the more blessings I receive.

_____

May my faith be multiplied, enabling me to face any obstacles, failures, or fears that come my way today. I pray that I remain focused on my faith throughout the day, in Jesus' name. AMEN

Personal Prayers Journal

....

....

....

....

....

....

....

....

Day 18

*"**For everyone who has been born of God overcomes the world**. And this is the victory that has overcome the world; our faith" (1 John 5:4).*

The beauty and blessing of receiving Jesus Christ as my Lord and Savior is experiencing abundant life in Him. Through my salvation, I also receive the victory to overcome life's stressors. This victory is based on the faith of the one who controls the day.

_____

May I receive the anointing of an overcomer to face any obstacles that may come my way today. May mountains be flattened and valleys be filled as I step out in faith today, in Jesus' Name. AMEN.

Personal Prayers Journal

....

....

....

....

....

....

Day 19

"Who brings forth his fruit in his season, and whatsoever he doeth shall prosper" (Psalms 1:3).

When I partner with God, He guarantees my divine provision, prosperity, and fruitfulness. He ensures divine favor and timing, removing every obstacle and delay that may come in the way of actualizing His word in my life.

Today, may I step into my season of fruitfulness and prosperity. I will eliminate all obstacles and delays from my path, and in Jesus' name, I will prosper in all that I do. AMEN.

Personal Prayers Journal

....

....

....

....

....

....

....

....

Day 20

"And it shall be, that the man who kills him, will receive great riches from the king, marry his daughter, and his entire father's house will live tax free in Israel" (1 Samuel 17:25).

Partnership with God brings me before kings and royalty. David experienced three-fold blessings in just one day after he took a stand and confronted the enemy of God.

———————————

May I experience multiple testimonies in virtues, values, and valuables today as I stand for Christ, honesty, and integrity today and always, in Jesus' name. AMEN.

Personal Prayers Journal

....

....

....

....

....

....

....

....

Day 21

*"**And God remembered Rachel,** and God hearkened to her, and opened her womb" (Genesis 30:22).*

There is a turnaround in lifelong unpleasant situations and circumstances when God divinely remembers me. He removes and replaces my reproach and shame with testimonies.

May the book of remembrance be opened to favor me today by releasing all delayed and detained blessings, in Jesus' Name, AMEN.

Personal Prayers Journal

....

....

....

....

....

....

....

....

....

Day 22

*"And God remembered Rachel, **and God hearkened to her, and opened her womb**" (Genesis 30:22).*

Testimony accompanies a divine visitation from God. The Lord heard, remembered, and answered Rachel when she called on Him with the birth of Joseph.

May heaven hear, answer and grant all my requests. May every shut womb be opened with physical and spiritual fertility to bear good and great fruits, and may I be remembered today, in Jesus Name, AMEN.

Personal Prayers Journal

....

....

....

....

....

....

....

....

....

Day 23

*"Go, gather together all the Jews that are present in Shushan, and fast ye for me, and neither eat nor drink three days, night or day: **I also and my maidens will fast likewise**; and so will I go in unto the king, which is not according to the law: and if I perish, I perish" (Esther 4:16).*

Corporate anointing releases torrents of testimonies. The grace to fast and stand in the gap for others opens the door for supernatural favor and divine access.

May the favor of God reverse the enemy's plan for my good. May God overturn every negative plan of the enemy to stop my lifting into prominence. May doors of favor be divinely accessible to me today, in Jesus' Name, AMEN.

Personal Prayers Journal

....

....

....

....

....

....

Day 24

*"Go, gather together all the Jews that are present in Shushan, and fast ye for me, and neither eat nor drink three days, night or day: I also and my maidens will fast likewise; **and so will I go in unto the king, which is not according to the law**: and if I perish, I perish"* (Esther 4:16).

An audience with God through fasting and prayers releases the boldness to open physical doors for me to experience on time advancement and increase.

———————————

May the elements of nature corporate with me as my step of faith moves me to the place of divine favor and attention of men against barriers of longstanding protocols and rules today, in Jesus Name, AMEN.

Personal Prayers Journal

....

....

....

....

....

....

Day 25

"I have swept away your offenses like a cloud, your sins like the morning mist. Return to me, for I have redeemed you"
(Isaiah 44:22).

There is power in the blood of Jesus to set us free from hatred, shame, and condemnation. The redeeming blood and Love of God have the ability to cleanse and remove any feelings of condemnation or shame.

_____

May the victorious redeeming love of Christ remove rejection, self-pity, shame, or condemnation from my life today, in Jesus' Name. AMEN.

Personal Prayers Journal

....

....

....

....

....

....

....

....

Day 26

"And the angel said unto her, Fear not, Mary: for thou hast found favor with God" (Luke1:30).

Angelic visitation not only removes fear but also positively announces my breakthrough and transformation. Just as the Angel was sent to Mary to reassure her and give her life-transforming news, may I receive angelic visitation today.

May the news I receive cause people to favor me. May this great good news be accompanied by joy and good tidings today, in Jesus' Name. AMEN.

Personal Prayers Journal

....

....

....

....

....

....

....

....

....

Day 27

"And thine ears shall hear a word behind thee, saying, this is the way, walk ye in it, when ye turn to the right hand, and when ye turn to the left" (Isaiah 30:21).

The voice of God, through His Holy Spirit, carries weight and power. There is nothing quite like hearing from God and being led by Him to the place of divine provision and blessing.

May today be the day of my Divine Visitation. May my spiritual antenna be alert and tuned to the right frequency, enabling me to hear the inaudible that directs me toward my breakthroughs today. May I receive the accurate word of life that will guide me to my divine allocation, blessings, and breakthroughs for today, in Jesus' Name. AMEN.

Personal Prayers Journal

....

....

....

....

....

....

Day 28

"I praise you because I am fearfully and wonderfully made"
(Psalms 139:14).

As God's creative masterpiece, we are created and designed to reign and rule with the divine intention of being a marvelous sight.

May the divine purpose of my creation be fulfilled today. The perfect God who created and designed me with accuracy will bring His purpose to fruition in my life today. I will experience and receive the blessings of His creation. My life will be a cause for others to praise God today, in Jesus' Name. AMEN.

Personal Prayers Journal

....

....

....

....

....

....

....

Day 29

"Behold, I stand at the door, and knock" (Revelation 3:20).

The spiritual access to God is open to all whose spirits connect with His. One must be spiritually awake and alert in order to hear the knock and open the door to allow Him in.

May my spiritual and physical ears be attentive to hear every door of opportunity that connects me to my greatness. May the wisdom to know what to do with this access be granted to me today, in Jesus' Name. AMEN.

Personal Prayers Journal

....

....

....

....

....

....

....

....

....

....

Day 30

"Then Adonijah the son of Haggith exalted himself, saying, I will be king" (1 Kings 1:5).

There is only one God, and He does not share His glory with another. God is also the one who appoints kings and dethrones them. I must wait for God to uplift me so that I don't end up like Adonijah, who desired to take someone else's position and suffered the consequences.

May the Lord protect me from any Adonijah-like schemes that could hinder my season of promotion. May I be elevated to the position I am destined for, as the Lord removes every obstacle and anything resembling an Adonijah in my life today, in Jesus' name. AMEN.

Personal Prayers Journal

....

....

....

....

....

....

Day 31

"And a certain man lame from his mother's womb was carried daily and laid at the temple gate he is Laid at the temple gate called Beautiful, to ask alms from anyone that enters into the temple" (Acts 3:2).

The extent of my influence and its potential are determined by the limitations and influence of my destiny helpers. Every day, the lame man was taken to the temple gate to beg because his helpers placed him there.

Today, I pray that any limitations in life that have hindered or made me dependent on others will be removed from my life. May my tale of sorrow be transformed into a collection of incredible testimonies as I encounter destiny helpers and gain the strength to stand up, jump, and dance my way into experiencing miracles today, in Jesus' name. AMEN.

Personal Prayers Journal

....

....

....

....

....

Day 32

*"And a certain man lame from his mother's womb was carried daily and laid at the temple gate **he is Laid at the temple gate called Beautiful, to ask alms from anyone that enters into the temple"** (Acts 3:2).*

My surroundings do not determine my vision and achievements in life. Even though the gate is described as beautiful, there was a lame man there asking for alms.

May every unpleasant situation and circumstance in my life be reversed and replaced with beautiful testimonies that will strengthen my faith today, in Jesus' Name.AMEN.

Personal Prayers Journal

....

....

....

....

....

....

....

....

Day 33

"Humble yourselves before the Lord, and he will lift you up in honor" (James 4:10).

Humility is a rare virtue that speaks for me even when I am silent. Submission and humility bring me into God's presence and elevate me to a place of honor among men

———————————

May the Lord help me to walk humbly before Him. May His hand lift me up before kings. May I not miss my opportunity for advancement as I step out today in Jesus' name. AMEN.

Personal Prayers Journal

....

....

....

....

....

....

....

....

....

....

Day 34

"And I will restore to you the years that the locust hath eaten, the cankerworm, and the caterpillar, and the palmerworm, my great army which I sent among you" (Joel 2:25).

A restored life experiences an acceleration and double blessings of what has been lost or missing. Christ is my restorer and He knows what is missing in my life.

May I receive complete and double restoration of unspeakable joy in every area of my life. May I receive divine speed of restoration as I run, overtake, and recover all lost possessions spiritually and physically today, in Jesus' Name. AMEN.

Personal Prayers Journal

....

....

....

....

....

....

....

....

Day 35

"Moses declared to Israel, every place where on the soles of your feet shall tread shall be yours" (Deut.11:24).

The word of God is declared to His Beloved and remains settled for eternity once spoken. I have a divine inheritance and access to everything the Lord has created.

Today, I declare that I will occupy all the spaces that God has reserved for me. May my space not be limited, but instead, may the Lord enlarge it. May His hand open locked doors and close revolving doors of stagnancy in my path today, in the Name of Jesus. AMEN.

Personal Prayers Journal

....

....

....

....

....

....

....

....

Day 36

"So the Lord was with Joshua; and his fame was noised throughout all the country" (Joshua 6:27).

The presence of the Lord is with me wherever I go and the presence of God in my life attracts grace, honor, favor and blessings.

_____

May the grace, glory of God be with me today and always. May it align my path to all my blessings and may the presence of God attract favor and honor to me as I step out today in, Jesus Name, AMEN.

Personal Prayers Journal

....

....

....

....

....

....

....

....

....

....

Day 37

*"So the Lord was with Joshua; **and his fame was noised throughout all the country**" (Joshua 6:27).*

The presence of God within me emanates His essence of dignity and fame to those around me. This very presence attracts others towards me, bringing blessings upon them.

May the radiance of His presence place me in advantageous positions. May the luminosity of His presence in my life be prominent as I emerge from obscurity into the spotlight starting from today, in Jesus' Name. AMEN

Personal Prayers Journal

....

....

....

....

....

....

....

....

Day 38

"But my God shall supply all your needs according to His riches in glory by Christ Jesus" (Philippians 4:19).

God is the sole source of all blessings, and He has the power to bestow upon me an abundanceof wealth and prosperity. He is capable of meeting all of my daily needs and providing for me in every way.

May there be an overflow of His abundance in both material riches and spiritual glory in my life. May I consistently enjoy a daily supply and provision of everything I can desire or envision, starting today, in Jesus' Name. AMEN.

Personal Prayers Journal

....

....

....

....

....

....

....

Day 39

*"**And I will make an everlasting covenant with them**, that I will not turn away from them, to do them good; but I will put my fear in their hearts, that they shall not depart from me"* *(Jeremiah 32:40).*

God is an eternal covenant keeper who honors His word above His name. He does not change; instead, He prioritizes me and fulfills all His promises for me as His covenant child.

May I receive the everlasting covenant promise of abundant life, peace, joy, and unending blessings. May God find me faithful to establish a life-transforming covenant with Him today, in Jesus' Name. AMEN.

Personal Prayers Journal

....

....

....

....

....

....

....

Day 40

*"And I will make an everlasting covenant with them, that **I will not turn away from them, to do them good**; but I will put my fear in their hearts, that they shall not depart from me"*
(Jeremiah 32:40).

God is a covenant-keeping God who honors His word above His name. His word becomes binding as soon as He declares it.

———————————————

May His declaration of goodness never depart from me. May the Lord not turn His eyes away from me. May His divine presence and goodness elevate me before Kings and not ordinary men. May all His goodness accompany me throughout today, in Jesus' Name, AMEN.

Personal Prayers Journal

....

....

....

....

....

....

Day 41

"And I will make an everlasting covenant with them, that I will not turn away from them, to do them good; **but I will put my fear in their hearts, that they shall not depart from me"** *(Jeremiah 32:40).*

The fear of the Lord is a reverential fear; it is an acknowledgment of His sovereignty and a way for me to draw close to Him. As I draw closer to God, I also become more like Him.

I pray that I may discover the fullness and pleasures of His presence as I draw closer to Jesus every day. May the reassurance and experience of intimacy with the Father fill my heart with His love today and always, in Jesus' name. AMEN.

Personal Prayers Journal

....

....

....

....

....

....

Day 42

"You have shown me the path of life" (Psalms 16:11).

The ultimate benefit of having a relationship with God is that He leads me each day on the right path.

May the Lord guide me in a divine way, revealing to me and bringing to fruition everything He has prepared for my eternal success, endless joy, and a peaceful existence like a river, today and every day, in Jesus' Name. AMEN.

Personal Prayers Journal

....

....

....

....

....

....

....

....

....

....

Day 43

"In your presence is fullness of joy, at your right hand are pleasures forevermore" (Psalms 16:11).

God is the ultimate source of joy and brings about indescribable joy when we are following His will. His right hand supports me every day.

―――――――――――――

May my joy be complete as I remain in His presence. May I experience full and multiplied restoration of joy in every aspect of my life, and may no one who tries to steal my joy come across my path as I go about my day today, in Jesus' name. AMEN.

Personal Prayers Journal

....

....

....

....

....

....

....

....

Day 44

*"**Arise, shine; for thy light is come**, and the glory of the LORD is risen upon thee" (Isaiah 60:1).*

To arise means to transition from a state of stagnation, limitation, and confinement into a state of motion. I am constantly grateful for His grace and favor, which shines upon me wherever I go.

May the voice of the Lord enable me to arise and shine in glory and victory over any illness, sadness, or sorrow from today onward, in Jesus' Name. AMEN

Personal Prayers Journal

....

....

....

....

....

....

....

....

....

Day 45

*"Arise, shine; for thy light is come, **and the glory of the LORD is risen upon thee***" (Isaiah 60:1).

The glory of God is an unmistakable fragrance that cannot be overlooked. It distinguishes and sets apart individuals, making them exceptional. It serves as a means to display myself to the world.

May His glorious presence be evident in me and radiate through me. May I emerge from obscurity and step into the spotlight. May the Lord receive honor and praise through everything I do today. As I embark on this day with joy and gratitude, it will culminate in a song of praise, in Jesus' Name. AMEN.

Personal Prayers Journal

....

....

....

....

....

....

Day 46

"And a voice from heaven said, "This is My beloved Son, in whom I am well pleased!" (Matthew 3:17)

Validation promotes positive actions and acknowledges the source of your influence. It also attracts more blessings and instills confidence in the constant presence of God.

May God's voice and presence support me in all my endeavors. May the window of heaven release a multitude of blessings upon me. May everything I do be pleasing and enjoyable to both God and others. May His glory and love shine through me, drawing others to Christ today, in Jesus' Name. Amen.

Personal Prayers Journal

....

....

....

....

....

....

....

Day 47

"The Queen of Sheba said to Solomon, because the Lord loved Israel for ever, therefore made he thee king" (1 Kings.10:9).

Israel is a nation that God has made a covenant with, and He is fiercely protective of them. No one can bring harm to someone whom God has chosen to bless. He appoints kings to fulfill His purpose and bring blessings to me.

———————————

I pray that the Lord recognizes me as a deserving, willing, and valuable instrument for His work. May He use me as a means of spreading blessings to the people of my generation, both in the present and for eternity, in Jesus' Name. AMEN.

Personal Prayers Journal

....

....

....

....

....

....

....

....

Day 48

"I remain confident of this: I will see the goodness of the LORD in the land of the living" (Psalms 27:13).

Confidence in God, who faithfully fulfills all His promises, assures and empowers us to trust in Him for successful outcomes and the achievement of our goals.

———————————————

May the confidence and assurance of my faith lead me to experience all the goodness and promises that God has for my life today, in Jesus' Name. AMEN

Personal Prayers Journal

....

....

....

....

....

....

....

....

....

Day 49

*"So the LORD was with Joshua; **and his fame was noised throughout all the country**" (Joshua 6:27).*

When it is time for someone's divine lifting, no man has any say in the matter. God's presence in the life of Joshua created a platform of prominence for him.

Today, may I be handpicked for a generational blessing. May the sound of my lifting be proclaimed across the nations. May it be said about me… "here comes the favored and blessed of the Lord" and may every noise of opposition be silenced today and forever in Jesus Name, AMEN.

Personal Prayers Journal

....

....

....

....

....

....

....

....

Day 50

*"**And he changeth the times and the seasons**: he removeth kings, and setteth up kings: he giveth wisdom unto the wise, and knowledge to them that know understanding"*
(Daniel 2:21).

God is the only one who has the authority to change the timing of events in a person's life. He can reverse or fast forward time and even stop it altogether, allowing me to fully embrace and enjoy my season of growth.

———————————————

May every period of change bring favor and blessings into my life. May my progress never be stagnant, reversed, or slow. May each new season bring refreshing and abundant blessings to me each day. I pray that today marks the start of a joyful season for me as I step forward in Jesus' name. AMEN.

Personal Prayers Journal

....

....

....

....

....

Day 51

*"And he changeth the times and the seasons: **he removeth kings, and setteth up kings**: he giveth wisdom unto the wise, and knowledge to them that know understanding"*
(Daniel 2:21).

God is the only one with the authority to appoint or dethrone anyone. His seal of approval is confirmed through successful reign and the accompanying positions of power and authority.

May the King of Kings be the one in charge of all my affairs. May The King of Kings take charge and place me on the throne of relevance, influence, affluence, and visibility today. May any king sitting on my blessings be dethroned today, in Jesus' Name, AMEN.

Personal Prayers Journal

....

....

....

....

....

Day 52

*"And he changeth the times and the seasons: he removeth kings, and setteth up kings: **he giveth wisdom unto the wise, and knowledge to them that know understanding"***
(Daniel 2:21).

Wisdom is the key to understanding and knowledge. It opens great doors for those who possess such virtue.

May the Lord fill me with wisdom and knowledge, enabling me to be a solution to the problems of others. May I be blessed with the grace to lead others to the knowledge of Christ. May His grace and goodness remain with me today and always, in Jesus' name, AMEN.

Personal Prayers Journal

....

....

....

....

....

....

....

Day 53

*"**Be careful for nothing;** but in every thing by prayer and supplication with thanksgiving let your requests be made known unto God" (Philippians 4:6).*

Anxiety has the power to leave us feeling stuck, restricted, and powerless. However, a life that embraces God's presence guarantees peace, joy, and overall tranquility.

May God's peace eradicate any anxiety within me. May I find solace in the Lord, knowing that He will provide for all my needs. May He bless me with good health, strength, and prosperity, allowing me to thrive and spread positivity in every aspect of my life. In Jesus' name, I pray. AMEN.

Personal Prayers Journal

....

....

....

....

....

....

....

Day 54

*"Be careful for nothing; **but in every thing by prayer and supplication with thanksgiving** let your requests be made known unto God" (Philippians 4:6).*

A heart filled with gratitude never lacks anything, as it opens more doors for blessings. A grateful attitude attracts more than a disgruntled expression.

———————————

May my barn be full and overflow. May I prosper greatly and become a blessing to a thousand generations, as my sacrifice of praise and thanksgiving ascends to heaven today, in Jesus' name. AMEN.

Personal Prayers Journal

....

....

....

....

....

....

....

....

Day 55

*"Be careful for nothing; but in every thing by prayer and supplication with thanksgiving **let your requests be made known unto God**" (Philippians 4:6).*

Your access to God is determined by your connection to Him. Just like the intimate relationship between a father and a child, it allows for unlimited access and audience at all times.

May my access to the Father never be restricted. May answers overflow as I present my requests to Him. May my case be given priority for answers even while I am still speaking. May there be a multiplication of good news and testimonies as I come before His presence today, in Jesus' Name, AMEN.

Personal Prayers Journal

....

....

....

....

....

....

....

Day 56

"But blessed are your eyes, for they see: and your ears, for they hear" (Matthew 13:16).

God's way of blessing me includes a supernatural awakening where my spiritual eyes and ears are opened to see the invisible and hear the inaudible.

———————————

May my eyes not be dim like Eli's. May I not stumble in spiritual darkness. May my spiritual antenna be tuned to God's heavenly frequency. May the Lord anoint my eyes afresh to have deep insight and revelation into the mysteries of the kingdom. May I have privileged insight into the mind of the Father today and always, in Jesus' Name, AMEN.

Personal Prayers Journal

....

....

....

....

....

....

....

Day 57

"And the third day there was a marriage in Cana, Jesus, His mother, and his disciples were invited to the marriage" *(John 2:1-2).*

A regular day can turn into an extraordinary day when there is a divine visitation. The presence of the Lord Jesus within me brings about divine intervention, attraction, and global recognition, as well as testimonies, resources, and blessings for me.

May I draw divine attention and favor, along with life-altering testimonies and abundance, as I invite Jesus to accompany me today. In Jesus' Name, AMEN.

Personal Prayers Journal

....
....
....
....
....
....
....

Day 58

"David says of the Lord, but you, Lord, are a shield around me, my glory, the One who lifts my head high" (Psalms 3:3)

Divine protection and an impenetrable covering are assured by the almighty God as my shield. He promises to fulfill the desires of my heart when I submit to Him.

The Lord almighty will be my shield and keep me safe from all my enemies. He will cover me with His glory, so I will not be ashamed. The Lord will raise my head above any reproach or false accusations made by my enemies. Today, I will proclaim His praise throughout the day. In Jesus' name, AMEN.

Personal Prayers Journal

....

....

....

....

....

....

....

Day 59

"But the meek shall inherit the earth; and shall delight themselves in the abundance of peace" (Psalms 37:11).

Humility is a virtue that attracts blessings from God and from others. By living a humble and fully devoted life to God, I am able to experience honorable opportunities.

As I embrace humility, may the Lord take pleasure in me, grant me peace, and fill my heart with joy. May others be drawn to the magnificent presence of God within me today, in Jesus' Name. AMEN.

Personal Prayers Journal

....

....

....

....

....

....

....

....

....

Day 60

"Howbeit the Lord would not destroy the house of David, because of the covenant that he had made with David"
(2 Chronicles 21:7).

The Lord testifies to the faithfulness of His faithful and is a covenant-keeping God who honors His word above His name.

May the Lord delight Himself in me. May the Lord bring me into a personal covenant relationship with Him. May His abundant mercies on me transcend to future generations, starting today, in Jesus' Name, AMEN.

Personal Prayers Journal

....

....

....

....

....

....

....

....

Day 61

"Then Samuel took the horn of oil, and anointed him in the midst of his brethren: and the Spirit of the LORD came upon David from that day forward. So Samuel rose up, and went to Ramah" (1 Samuel 16:13).

Anointing invites the Holy Spirit into someone's life and bestows favor, mercy, and grace upon believers.

May the oil of joy and gladness never cease to flow over me. May His presence remain with me. May my enemies be present to witness my elevation and upliftment. May every opposition be silenced and rendered powerless as my blessings overflow, displaying His glory from this day forward. In Jesus' name, AMEN.

Personal Prayers Journal

....

....

....

....

....

....

Day 62

"Then Samuel took the horn of oil, and anointed him in the midst of his brethren: and the Spirit of the LORD came upon David from that day forward. So Samuel rose up, and went to Ramah" (1 Samuel 16:13).

The anointing of the Holy Spirit on His beloved is a public confirmation of His divine ownership and a clear announcement to the world.

Lord, allow me to see the manifestation of Your blessings and uplifting today, in the presence of others. May the anointing oil upon me attract favor for advancement and divine speed for breakthroughs and greatness, in Jesus' Name, amen.

Personal Prayers Journal

....

....

....

....

....

....

....

Day 63

"Then Samuel took the horn of oil, and anointed him in the midst of his brethren: **and the Spirit of the LORD came upon David from that day forward. So Samuel rose up, and went to Ramah"** *(1 Samuel 16:13).*

There is a positive shift and transformation in the life of anyone who encounters God and carries the anointing of the Holy Spirit.

——————————————

May my transformation and elevation be immediate. May every spirit of delay be removed from my path. May the Spirit of God come upon me, abide with me, and guide me continually. May the Spirit of God be evident in my life as I step out today, in Jesus' Name, AMEN.

Personal Prayers Journal

....

....

....

....

....

....

Day 64

*"**And the LORD shall guide thee continually, and satisfy thy soul in drought**, and make fat thy bones: and thou shalt be like a watered garden, and like a spring of water, whose waters fail not" (Isaiah 58:11).*

The Lord is the ultimate guide for those in need of divine direction because He not only knows the way, but He is also the creator of it.

May the Lord hold my hands and lead me to the place where my blessings await. May He direct my steps so that I do not lose my way or stumble along the journey. With divine guidance, I am confident that I will not falter. Today, I pray that my soul shall be completely satisfied with His grace and goodness. In Jesus' name, AMEN.

Personal Prayers Journal

....

....

....

....

....

....

Day 65

*"And the LORD shall guide thee continually, and satisfy thy soul in drought, **and make fat thy bones: and thou shalt be like a watered garden, and like a spring of water, whose waters fail not**" (Isaiah 58:11).*

A tree that is planted by the rivers of water never experiences drought because water is a source of life.

May my life resemble a watered garden that flourishes, rejuvenates, and regenerates daily. I will never experience drought or dryness. May my bones be made strong, and may I never be weak. May I increase abundantly, and may my seasonal garden continue to draw from the endless streams of joy and gladness from today and forever, in Jesus' Name, AMEN.

Personal Prayers Journal

....

....

....

....

....

....

Day 66

"Behold what manner of love the Father has bestowed on us that we should be called the children of God" (1 John 3:1).

The privilege of connecting and relating to God as a Father and son is a perfect example of His unconditional love for me. However, it is important to note that not everyone is considered a child of God.

———————————

May the unmistakable mark of divine ownership be evident in me. May strangers look upon me with favor, and may great men and kings honor me. As I step out today, I declare that I will not be pulled down or experience shame or rejection. I claim this victory in Jesus' name, AMEN.

Personal Prayers Journal

....

....

....

....

....

....

....

Day 67

"Let them shout for joy and be filled who favor my righteous cause; and let them say continually, let the Lord be magnified"
(Psalms 35:27).

The victorious side is always the joyous side. By raising my voice in praise to God, I thwart any plans of the devil to upset me.

Today, the Lord will eliminate any worry, burden, or trouble from my life. May I have reasons to shout for joy and may my heart be filled with songs of praise and gratitude as I step out today, in Jesus' Name, AMEN.

Personal Prayers Journal

....

....

....

....

....

....

Day 68

"Let the Lord be Magnified who has pleasure in the prosperity of His servant" (Psalms 35:27).

A good father finds joy and takes pride in his children's success. The Lord rejoices when I experience overall prosperity.

Today, may my actions and choices please God. May they lead to growth and expansion in every aspect of my life. May the Lord always be pleased with everything I do, receiving praise from heaven. In Jesus' Name, AMEN.

Personal Prayers Journal

....

....

....

....

....

....

....

....

....

....

Day 69

"He revealed the deep and secret things: he knoweth what is in the darkness, and the light dwelleth with him" (Daniel 2:22).

God sees the contents of my heart and purges me with His light to remove all darkness and secret sins that seek to put me in bondage.

May the light of His presence in me reveal, overshadow, and remove any darkness surrounding me, and may the light of God reveal all hidden secrets that require immediate attention in my favor today, in Jesus' Name, AMEN.

Personal Prayers Journal

....

....

....

....

....

....

....

....

....

Day 70

"I thank thee, and praise thee, O thou God of my fathers, who hast given me wisdom and might, for thou hast now made known unto us the king's matter" (Daniel 2:23).

God rewards my holy and righteous lifestyle and shows up for me, just as He did for Daniel and his friends when they set themselves apart.

———————————

May I be rewarded with wisdom for serving God. May God rise up for me as I live a holy and righteous life. May I be positioned as a solution to the king's issues. May that divine wisdom guide me and place me in a position of prominence today, in Jesus' name. Amen.

Personal Prayers Journal

....

....

....

....

....

....

....

Day 71

"Delight yourself also in the Lord, and he shall give you the desires of your heart" (Psalms 37:4).

Delighting in a thankful and grateful heart opens doors for additional blessings. When my focus is on delighting in God, He takes pleasure in giving me more than I could ever desire, ask, or think.

_____

May my delight in God open great and influential doors for me. May all the desires of my heart, and more, be granted. May I be a recipient of divine opportunities for advancement today, in Jesus' Name, AMEN.

Personal Prayers Journal

....

....

....

....

....

....

....

....

Day 72

"Though he falls, he shall not be utterly cast down. For the Lord upholds him with His hand" (Psalms 37:24).

The mighty hand of God carries and sustains me, providing solid support through any storm of life. When the hand of God carries a person, they cannot fall or fail.

———————————————

May the hand of the Lord carry me above every storm and problem in life today. May the hand of the Lord protect me from the enemy's arrows and darts. May the hand of the Lord keep me firmly grounded on the solid rock of progress and seamless promotion as I embark on this day, in Jesus' Name, AMEN.

Personal Prayers Journal

....

....

....

....

....

....

....

Day 73

"Let them shout for joy, and be glad, that favour my righteous cause: yea, let them say continually, Let the Lord be magnified, **which hath pleasure in the prosperity of his servant"** *(Psalms 35:27).*

The Lord we serve is the richest in heaven and on earth. He takes pleasure in enriching me as His child every single day of my life.

———————————

May God's presence bring me what rightfully belongs to me. May all the blessings meant for today find their way to me. May I experience growth and expansion in every aspect of my life. May I never experience lack or have to beg for bread. And may all limitations be removed as I step into seasons of joy today and always, in Jesus' name, AMEN.

Personal Prayers Journal

....

....

....

....

....

....

Day 74

"I will make thy name to be remembered in all generations: therefore, shall the people praise thee for ever and ever"
(Psalms 45:17).

Divine promotion is granted by the Lord when He enables others to remember and support me, just as He did for Mordecai

---

May both heaven and earth remember me today. May the Lord send me helpers who will expedite my breakthrough and bring forth testimonies, in the name of Jesus. AMEN.

Personal Prayers Journal

....

....

....

....

....

....

....

....

Day 75

"Commit your way to the Lord; Trust also in Him, and He shall bring it to pass" (Psalms 37:5).

Trusting and walking with God brings great rewards because commitment and trust speed up my blessings and promotion.

May my diligence and trust hasten angelic response for divine intervention and testimonies in my favor. May I receive resolutions to all pending matters as the God of last-minute miracles remembers me today, in Jesus' Name, AMEN.

Personal Prayers Journal

....

....

....

....

....

....

....

....

....

Day 76

"The steps of a good man are ordered by God, and He delights in his way" (Psalms 37:23).

I cannot be led astray when I walk with God because His words and promises will guide my steps as I continually find joy in Him.

———————————————

May He find joy in me today. May His hands lead, guide, and direct me. May the Lord carry me through the storms, and may He show me the path to a life filled with abundance in Him today, in Jesus' name, AMEN.

Personal Prayers Journal

....

....

....

....

....

....

....

....

....

Day 77

"Thou art fairer than the children of men: grace is poured into thy lips: therefore God hath blessed thee forever" (Psalms 46:2).

God's blessings upon me unleash the grace to sustain and protect me in His secret place for eternity.

May men be drawn to show favor and bless me. May I be singled out for an unexpected promotion. May the fragrance of His grace attract kindness to me from all corners of the earth. Today, may I be known as the blessed of the Lord, in Jesus' Name, AMEN.

Personal Prayers Journal

....

....

....

....

....

....

....

....

....

Day 78

"Then shall thy light break forth as the morning, and thine health shall spring forth speedily: and thy righteousness shall go before thee; the glory of the LORD shall be thy rereward" (Isaiah 58:8).

The joy of a new dawn lies in the certainty of light. As the light emerges, the force of darkness and weakness surrenders, making room for the radiance of divine health and strength.

———————————————

May His light within me be apparent to everyone as I embark on this day. May people be attracted to my light. May the power of healing emanate from within me, reversing any illnesses and diseases in my life. May I walk in divine health starting today, in Jesus' name. AMEN.

Personal Prayers Journal

....

....

....

....

....

....

Day 79

*"Then shall thy light break forth as the morning, and thine health shall spring forth speedily: and **thy righteousness shall go before thee; the glory of the LORD shall be thy rereward**" (Isaiah 58:8).*

The Lord rewards those who are righteous and diligently seek Him. He watches over us like a pillar of fire and cloud every day.

―――――――――――――――

May God's glory go before me. May the book of remembrance be opened for my sake today. May I receive double blessings for the troubles I have faced. May today be a special time for blessings in my life. May any delays in my life be removed. May influential people rise to grant me the promotions I deserve today, in Jesus' name, AMEN.

Personal Prayers Journal

....

....

....

....

....

....

Day 80

"Then shalt thou call, and the LORD shall answer; thou shalt cry, and he shall say, Here I am. If thou take away from the midst of the yoke, the putting forth of the finger, and speaking vanity" (Isaiah 58:9).

God knows and recognizes the voice of all His beloved. He arises and comes to my aid when I raise my voice in supplication to Him.

―――――――――――――

May my voice be recognized in Heaven. May Heaven respond to my petition swiftly and divinely. May I receive answers to all the cries of my heart while I am still speaking, today, in Jesus' Name, AMEN.

Personal Prayers Journal

....

....

....

....

....

....

....

Day 81

*"Then shalt thou call, and the LORD shall answer; thou shalt cry, and he shall say, Here I am. **If thou take away from the midst of thee the yoke, the putting forth of the finger, and speaking vanity**" (Isaiah 58:9).*

Sin, iniquity, negativity, and ungodly lifestyle, and self-destructive words nullify the blessings of God over one's life.

———————————

May only words of edification, lifting, and blessings come out of my mouth today. May my spiritual eyes be opened to uproot any self-limiting, self-destructive self-condemnating and vain words hovering over me today, in Jesus' Name, AMEN.

Personal Prayers Journal

....

....

....

....

....

....

Day 82

*"**And the LORD shall guide thee continually**, and satisfy thy soul in drought, and make fat thy bones: and thou shalt be like a watered garden, and like a spring of water, whose waters fail not" (Isaiah 58:11).*

There is a difference when the Lord guides you compared to when you decide to walk alone without His presence.

———————————

May the Lord guide me and envelop me with His everlasting and loving arms. May His presence continuously lead, guide, direct, and pave the way for me on the right path today, in Jesus' Name, AMEN.

Personal Prayers Journal

....

....

....

....

....

....

....

....

Day 83

*"And the LORD shall guide thee continually, **and satisfy thy soul in drought**, and make fat thy bones: and thou shalt be like a watered garden, and like a spring of water, whose waters fail not" (Isaiah 58:11).*

God is the one who quenches the thirsty soul. He has the living water that flows ceaselessly to satisfy any thirst.

May the Lord satisfy my thirst with the rivers of Living Water that never run dry. May I flourish and bear fruit that edifies and multiplies daily. May I experience seasons of fertility in every area of drought from today, in Jesus' Name. AMEN.

Personal Prayers Journal

....

....

....

....

....

....

....

....

Day 84

*"And the LORD shall guide thee continually, and satisfy thy soul in drought, **and make fat thy bones**: and thou shalt be like a watered garden, and like a spring of water, whose waters fail not" (Isaiah 58:11).*

We serve a God who can provide for all of my needs. I will never go hungry or beg for bread because the silver and gold belong to Him, and He knows what I need even before I ask.

As I go about my day, may the Lord bless me with unlimited resources. May I never struggle or barely survive in life. May I experience growth and prosperity in every aspect. May I always enjoy the abundance of this land, in the name of Jesus, AMEN.

Personal Prayers Journal

....

....

....

....

....

....

Day 85

*"And the LORD shall guide thee continually, and satisfy thy soul in drought, and make fat thy bones: **and thou shalt be like a watered garden, and like a spring of water, whose waters fail not**" (Isaiah 58:11).*

A connection to the source of life ensures an abundant and endless flow of living waters that are not restricted by seasons but blossom all year round.

As I connect to the Sustainer of life today, may I overflow on all sides. May my connection to Jesus not be tampered with, disconnected, severed, or abruptly terminated. May I not experience power failure or power surge that interrupts the flow. May the enemies not slow down my journey through distractions, in Jesus' Name, AMEN.

Personal Prayers Journal

....

....

....

....

....

....

Day 86

"Surely goodness and mercy shall follow me all the days of my life, and I will dwell in the house of the Lord forever" (Psalms 23:6).

The word "surely" not only assures but also confirms the accurate fulfillment of a promise from the only true God who watches over every word to perform it.

Without a doubt, the Lord will expedite the promise of His goodness and mercy over my life. I will fulfill the divine mandate of accelerated progress with multiple-fold increase. The manifestation of His goodness and mercy in my life will no longer be delayed from today, in Jesus' Name, AMEN.

Personal Prayers Journal

....

....

....

....

....

....

....

Day 87

*"Surely goodness and mercy shall follow me all the days of my life, and **I will dwell in the house of the Lord forever**"*
(Psalms 23:6).

Access to the presence of God is a promise for all of God's children, ensuring they can always be with Him. This promise guarantees permanent access to abide with Him forever.

May I have immediate access to the throne room of grace today, and may the key to unlock great doors be granted to me. I pray that I will never leave Your divine presence. Lord, may my ways always be pleasing to You, in Jesus' name. AMEN.

Personal Prayers Journal

....

....

....

....

....

....

....

Day 88

"Then shalt thou delight thyself in the LORD; and I will cause thee to ride upon the high places of the earth, and feed thee with the heritage of Jacob thy father: for the mouth of the LORD hath spoken it" (Isaiah 58:14).

A delightful heart and countenance attract divine visitation, causing people to favor and elevate me to a place of honor and royalty.

As I come before God today, may I receive direct access to the throne room of grace. May my journey to the top be smooth and effortless. May today be the least I will ever be as the Lord removes any obstacle to my greatness today, in Jesus' name amen.

Personal Prayers Journal

....

....

....

....

....

....

....

Day 89

*"Then shalt thou delight thyself in the LORD; and I will cause thee to ride upon the high places of the earth, **and feed thee with the heritage of Jacob thy father: for the mouth of the LORD hath spoken it**" (Isaiah 58:14).*

One of Jacob's legacies is the covenant of generational blessings. I am a beneficiary of Jacob's promise because God's word is permanently established in my life.

———————————

May I encounter divine expansion and growth on a daily basis. May my descendants become prosperous contributors to society as the Lord begins to bring about its exact fulfillment in my favor today, in Jesus' Name, AMEN.

Personal Prayers Journal

....

....

....

....

....

....

....

Day 90

"I will instruct thee and teach thee in the way which thou shalt go: I will guide thee with mine eye" (Psalms 32:8).

Obedience to God's divine leading and directions ensures safety, peace, and joy. It gives me the assurance that I cannot lose my way when God is the one instructing me.

_____

May my steps be divinely directed. May the Lord hold my hand and guide me. May I hear His still, small voice as He teaches, instructs, and directs me to the paths of life and success today, in Jesus' Name, AMEN.

Personal Prayers Journal

....

....

....

....

....

....

....

....

Day 91

*"I will instruct thee and teach thee in the way which thou shalt go: **I will guide thee with mine eye**" (Psalms 32:8).*

The eyes of the Lord bring illumination and dispel all darkness. When His eyes are my guide, my understanding is enlightened to perceive beyond the physical realm.

May my understanding be enlightened, and may I never be blind to spiritual matters. May I be shielded from oppression, delay, or denial. May His guidance prevent me from stumbling into the snares and pitfalls set by my adversaries today, in the name of Jesus, AMEN.

Personal Prayers Journal

....

....

....

....

....

....

Day 92

*"**Arise, shine; for thy light is come**, and the glory of the LORD is risen upon thee" (Isaiah 60:1).*

The commandment for me to arise and shine causes me to transition from a state of stagnancy to the movement of God's light that sets me apart.

———————————————

May His light set me apart and bring blessings into my life. May I never walk in darkness as His light shines through me. May my light shine brighter and brighter every day. May all forms of darkness fade away from this moment onwards in Jesus name, amen.

Personal Prayers Journal

....

....

....

....

....

....

....

....

Day 93

*"Arise, shine; for thy light is come, **and the glory of the LORD is risen upon thee**" (Isaiah 60:1).*

The glory of God distinguishes me from others and sets me apart. It results in others favoring me physically.

May His presence and glory remain with me every day. May His glory bring me before kings and not ordinary men. Today, I pray for a tangible and positive manifestation of His glory. In Jesus' Name, AMEN.

Personal Prayers Journal

....

....

....

....

....

....

....

....

....

Day 94

"O clap your hands, all ye people; shout unto God with the voice of triumph" (Psalms 47:1).

A joyful heart, with shouts of praise, lifting hands, is the key to the open door and direct access into the presence of the Father.

As I enter His presence, rejoicing and singing songs of praise, may the Lord come and visit me. He will sing and rejoice over me, sustaining, strengthening, and sanctifying me. May triumphant shouts of victory be heard in my home today, in Jesus' Name. AMEN.

Personal Prayers Journal

....

....

....

....

....

....

....

....

Day 95

*"**Then Samuel took a vial of oil, and poured it upon his head**, and kissed him, and said, is it not because the LORD hath anointed thee to be captain over his inheritance"*
(1 Samuel 10: 1).

Anointing is the physical affirmation of God's presence on His chosen ones, transforming an ordinary season into an extraordinary one

---

May the Lord anoint me as His chosen one, and may the oil upon my head overflow. May the manifestation of His presence in my life be evident to everyone. May my spiritual elevation begin today, and may all those who can assist me show up to provide favor, in Jesus' Name, AMEN.

Personal Prayers Journal

....

....

....

....

....

....

Day 96

"And the speech pleased the Lord, that Solomon had asked this thing" (1 Kings 3:10).

The tongue of the righteous is like precious silver. It carries anointing, power, and is pleasing to those who hear it.

May my voice be a delightful fragrance filled with praises that bring forth abundant blessings from heaven. May my words capture the attention of the heavenly hosts and prompt angelic responses, bringing forth answers and solutions to long-awaited good news today, in Jesus' name. Amen.

Personal Prayers Journal

....

....

....

....

....

....

....

....

....

Day 97

"Then Samuel took a vial of oil, and poured it upon his head, **and kissed him, and said, is it not because the LORD hath anointed thee to be captain over his inheritance"** *(1 Samuel 10: 1).*

God's anointing attracts prominence and divine favor that cannot be contested by all my friends and enemies.

May the oil of greatness on my head become visible manifestations of blessings. May all opposition to my promotion be rendered powerless, and may my inheritance be handed over to me today, in Jesus' Name, AMEN.

Personal Prayers Journal

....

....

....

....

....

....

....

Day 98

*"**Death and life are in the power of the tongue**: and they that love it shall eat the fruit thereof" (Proverbs 18:21).*

TThe tongue is a powerful tool for blessing, proclaiming liberty to the oppressed, and reversing every sentence of death in my life. It is said that a closed mouth is a closed destiny.

As I open my mouth, may the Lord fill it with wisdom, knowledge, and understanding. May my words not fall to the ground empty, but instead accomplish all that they are sent to do. May my words of life attract people to the light of God for salvation today, in Jesus' Name, AMEN.

Personal Prayers Journal

....

....

....

....

....

....

....

....

Day 99

"As soon as I heard your voice of greetings, the baby in my womb leaped for joy" (Luke 1:44).

Leaping is an action that involves sudden forward motion, symbolizing the arrival of positive news that brings joy and happiness.

May God guide me to transition from a state of stagnation to rapid and sudden progress. I anticipate multiple promotions in my future. Today, as I venture forth, I pray that my season of physical and spiritual limitations comes to an end. I step out with the expectation of receiving a double portion, in Jesus' Name, AMEN.

Personal Prayers Journal

....

....

....

....

....

....

....

Day 100

*"**And the maiden pleased him, and she obtained kindness of him**; and he speedily gave her her things for purification, with such things as belonged to her, and seven maidens, which were meet to be given her, out of the king's house: and he preferred her and her maids unto the best place of the house of the women" (Esther 2:9).*

The presence of God's glory in any of His children attracts favor. With God's glory, Esther presented herself among others and was favored.

———————————————

May my presence in the throne room be pleasing to God today. May everyone I come across show me kindness. May I be preferred among others, and may strangers arise to favor me from today, in Jesus' Name, AMEN.

Personal Prayers Journal

....

....

....

....

....

....

Day 101

"For they being ignorant of God's righteousness, and going about to establish their own righteousness, have not submitted themselves unto the righteousness of God" (Romans 10:3).

A self-righteous lifestyle leads to pride. However, walking in holiness and righteousness is a consecration to God alone.

I pray that I never struggle but continue to have direct access to His presence as I daily walk in holiness, righteousness, and truth. May I experience the countless blessings that come with complete submission to God. May my intimate relationship with the Lord grow stronger every day. In Jesus' name, AMEN.

Personal Prayers Journal

....

....

....

....

....

....

....

Day 102

"And the maiden pleased him, and she obtained kindness of him; **and he speedily gave her her things for purification, with such things as belonged to her,** *and seven maidens, which were meet to be given her, out of the king's house: and he preferred her and her maids unto the best place of the house of the women"* (Esther 2:9).

A person who possesses the grace and glory of God naturally attracts favor. The mere presence of His fragrance makes people exceedingly kind to me at all times.

May my life continuously draw favor from both God and men. May everything that is rightfully mine be released into my hands today. May people come forward to support me in reaching the pinnacle. May I move with divine speed from this day forward as I run, overtake, and reclaim everything that is rightfully mine, in Jesus' Name, AMEN.

Personal Prayers Journal

....

....

....

....

Day 103

*"And the maiden pleased him, and she obtained kindness of him; and he speedily gave her her things for purification, with such things as belonged to her, **and seven maidens, which were meet to be given her, out of the king's house**: and he preferred her and her maids unto the best place of the house of the women" (Esther 2:9).*

The significance of the number of maidens given to Esther was accurately fulfilled, as she proved to be the perfect choice for the position and a suitable match for the King she married.

As seven is considered a number of perfection, I believe that the Lord will perfect everything that concerns me. Today, in Jesus' name, may the Lord bless me seven-fold with favor, honor, promotion, elevation, royalty, lifting, and divine preference, AMEN.

Personal Prayers Journal

....

....

....

....

....

Day 104

"For I know the thoughts that I think toward you, saith the LORD, thoughts of peace, and not of evil, to give you an expected end" (Jeremiah 29:11).

I am reminded of God's daily thoughts towards me, as He lovingly formed and cares for me as His child.

———————————

May His perfect plan for my life be fully realized. May my destiny not be hindered, disrupted, or cut short. May any opposing force that is causing delays in my life be removed. May Heaven graciously shower me with blessings today, in the name of Jesus, AMEN.

Personal Prayers Journal

....

....

....

....

....

....

....

....

Day 105

"And they that shall be of thee shall build the old waste places: thou shalt raise up the foundations of many generations; and thou shalt be called, the repairer of the breach, The restorer of paths to dwell in" (Isaiah 58:12).

Foundations are crucial for a building to be strong and durable. A flawed foundation is unable to support a structure or withstand the passage of time.

As I remain firmly anchored to the unwavering foundation of Christ, may the Lord grant me wisdom to bring blessings for future generations. May my descendants become providers for nations as I walk with a clear sense of purpose. May I tread on steady ground, void of any faults or instability. Wherever I step today will be my Rehoboth, the place where I receive my inheritance and prosperity, in Jesus' name, AMEN.

Personal Prayers Journal

....

....

....

....

....

Day 106

*"And they that shall be of thee shall build the old waste places: thou shalt raise up the foundations of many generations; and **thou shalt be called, the repairer of the breach, The restorer of paths to dwell in**" (Isaiah 58:12).*

My name holds great significance and plays a crucial role in fulfilling my destiny. I am filled with joy knowing that the Lord refers to me as His child, not as a slave.

May my name serve as a symbol of greatness and success. May it strike fear into the heart of the devil and be associated with the restoration of lives. May it also become synonymous with joy, peace, and favor from this day forward. In Jesus' name, I pray, AMEN.

Personal Prayers Journal

....

....

....

....

....

....

Day 107

*"**And it came to pass, before he had done speaking, that, behold, Rebekah came out,** who was born to Bethuel, son of Milcah, the wife of Nahor, Abraham's brother, with her pitcher upon her shoulder" (Genesis 24:15).*

I serve a God who listens to every cry of my heart and is quick to respond, even as I am still making my request.

As I step out today, may the Lord answer me before I even speak. May all my requests become testimonies while I am still speaking, and may the heavens over my head be opened to receive multiple answers of God's best for me today, in Jesus' Name, AMEN.

Personal Prayers Journal

....

....

....

....

....

....

....

Day 108

*"**On that night could not the king sleep**, and he commanded to bring the book of records of the chronicles; and they were read before the king" (Esther 6:1).*

Kings and rulers are helpers of destiny whom God raises to meet my needs and promptly respond to my petitions.

When the time for my promotion comes, may King Ahaseurus lose sleep until he promotes me. May each of my destiny helpers be restless until they rise up to assist me. May I be elevated to a position of honor, dignity, and favor with great speed from God. May my enemies be powerless as I sit on my throne of success; may they be perplexed as I continue to climb the ladder of success starting today, in the name of Jesus, AMEN.

Personal Prayers Journal

....

....

....

....

....

Day 109

"Therefore God, thy God, hath anointed thee with the oil of gladness above thy fellows" (Psalms 45:7).

The anointing oil from God sets one apart from others. It elevates me above my peers, making me a marvel to myself and to them.

The Lord will anoint my hands for success, surpassing my contemporaries. My feet are anointed for progress; my eyes are anointed to perceive the unseen and the goodness of God in the land of the living. My ears are anointed to hear the unheard and only good news. My mouth is anointed to speak of God's blessings and abundant testimonies. My head is anointed for joy and filled with wisdom, knowledge, and understanding starting today, in the name of Jesus, AMEN.

Personal Prayers Journal

....

....

....

....

....

....

Day 110

*"**And he took the mantle of Elijah that fell from him, and smote the waters**, and said, Where is the LORD God of Elijah? And when he also had smitten the waters, they parted hither and thither: and Elisha went over" (2 Kings 2:14).*

The mantle symbolizes anointing, authority, and the staff of office. God is capable and willing to transfer a double portion of such anointing onto a consecrated vessel that has been tested and proven worthy.

———————————

May my mantle of greatness be bestowed upon me today, and may rivers part and mountains be leveled as I fulfill the role that is meant for me. May the mantle of a finisher be upon me today, in Jesus' Name, AMEN.

Personal Prayers Journal

....

....

....

....

....

....

Day 111

*"And he took the mantle of Elijah that fell from him, and smote the waters, **and said, where is the LORD God of Elijah?** And when he also had smitten the waters, they parted hither and thither: and Elisha went over"* (2 Kings 2:14).

There is power, grace, and authority in the words spoken by a vessel anointed by God who proclaims the gospel.

Today, as I open my mouth, the Lord will fill it with grace, power, and authority. May the response to my voice be accompanied by an accelerated response of answers. May all those who mock me bow before me in silence as heaven responds to every decree and declaration I make, in Jesus' Name, AMEN.

Personal Prayers Journal

....

....

....

....

....

....

Day 112

"And he took the mantle of Elijah that fell from him, and smote the waters, and said, where is the LORD God of Elijah? ***And when he also had smitten the waters, they parted hither and thither:*** *and Elisha went over"* (2 Kings 2:14).

Anointing with tenacity attracts the attention of Heaven. The anointing cannot remain inactive or concealed, but is unleashed through a lifestyle of holiness and righteousness.

May the grace to pursue, overtake, and recover everything the devil has taken from me be upon me today. May every barrier and hindrance in my life be removed immediately when I command, and may angelic hosts swiftly respond to all my prayers with an abundant supply of all that I request or envision today, in the Name of Jesus, AMEN.

Personal Prayers Journal

....

....

....

....

....

....

Day 113

*"And he took the mantle of Elijah that fell from him, and smote the waters, and said, where is the LORD God of Elijah? And when he also had smitten the waters, they parted hither and thither: **and Elisha went over**" (2 Kings 2:14).*

Stagnancy is a state of despair, despondency, and limitation. Taking a step of faith in the right direction will bring you closer to your life goal.

Just as Elisha entered into a new phase after receiving a double portion of anointing, I pray that I may also cross over into my own newness today. Today, I receive the double portion anointing to enter into my place of greatness, promotion, increase, and the very best that God has in store for me. In Jesus' name, AMEN.

Personal Prayers Journal

....

....

....

....

....

....

Day 114

"Jesus saith unto him, Rise, take up thy bed, and walk"
(John 5:8).

At the mention of the name Jesus, every knee shall bow and demons tremble.

———————————————

May I rise from any state of stagnation, limitation, and obscurity into the limelight. I declare that any affliction over me is removed by the blood of Jesus. May my steps be guided as I walk, run, overtake, and reclaim all the years I have lost. May all the areas of my life that have been unproductive and barren flourish and blossom with multiple blessings today, in Jesus' name, AMEN.

Personal Prayers Journal

....

....

....

....

....

....

....

Day 115

*"But a certain Samaritan, as he journeyed, came where he was: **and when he saw him, he had compassion on him**"*
(Luke 10:33).

A compassionate and loving heart brings joy and fulfillment to the lives of others. Sharing and spreading this joy creates a ripple effect that touches others deeply.

May I be granted the grace to love unconditionally. May my heart be filled with compassion. May my spiritual eyes be opened to the needs of others. May I receive the grace to become a generational asset and blessing to others today, in Jesus' Name, AMEN.

Personal Prayers Journal

....

....

....

....

....

....

....

Day 116

"And he went to him, and bound up his wounds, pouring in oil and wine, and set him on his own beast, and brought him to an inn, and took care of him" (Luke 10:34).

The God we serve is loving and compassionate. When we walk in love and have a compassionate heart, we will experience recognition and receive heavenly rewards.

May my life bring joy and fulfillment to others. May I receive abundant blessings for the challenges I face. May my acts of kindness towards others be noted in Heaven and be returned to me multiplied with blessings today, in Jesus' Name, AMEN.

Personal Prayers Journal

....

....

....

....

....

....

....

Day 117

*"**And ye shall serve the Lord your God, and he shall bless thy bread, and thy water,** and I will take sickness away from the midst of thee"* (Exodus 23:25).

My service to God is to reciprocate His love for me, and it opens the door to experiencing supernatural provision for all my needs.

May my service never be rejected, but instead be accepted as a pleasing offering. May the Lord provide me with spiritual sustenance, to make my service easier. May the Lord reward my service with access to generational blessings starting from today, in Jesus' Name, AMEN.

Personal Prayers Journal

....

....

....

....

....

....

....

Day 118

*"And ye shall serve the Lord your God, and he shall bless thy bread, and thy water, **and I will take sickness away from the midst of thee**". (Exodus 23:25).*

The covenant of divine health is established with all of God's children since Christ died on the cross to take away our sins, sicknesses, and shame.

As I step out today, may sickness and diseases be taken away from me. May I not be afflicted with any incurable diseases. May my body, which is the temple of the Holy Spirit, cast out any infirmities today, in Jesus' Name, AMEN.

Personal Prayers Journal

....

....

....

....

....

....

....

....

Day 119

"For in him we live, and move, and have our being; as certain also of your own poets have said, for we are also his offspring"
(Acts17:28).

Our salvation is a connection to the Lord Jesus, and the presence of the Holy Spirit within us serves as evidence of God's divine ownership.

———————————

Since I bear this mark of Christ through His blood, I declare that I am protected from any calamity or conspiracy that may hinder my progress. I am a formidable force and a threat to all who oppose me. May all those who seek to hinder my progress be rendered powerless and scattered in their own foolishness, as I continue to rise higher in grace, grandeur, and the glory of God today. In Jesus' name, AMEN.

Personal Prayers Journal

....

....

....

....

....

....

Day 120

*"**Fear thou not; for I am with thee**: be not dismayed; for I am thy God: I will strengthen thee; yea, I will help thee; yea, I will uphold thee with the right hand of my righteousness"* (Isaiah 41:10).

When the Lord's presence is within me, I am always assured of peace. His voice has the power to quiet all other voices, which is why I have no reason to be afraid.

As He has spoken about me today, may every voice of fear and frustration be permanently silenced. May His presence eradicate all fear and replace it with faith. I ask for the grace to move forward, overcome, and regain everything I have lost today, in Jesus' Name, AMEN.

Personal Prayers Journal

....

....

....

....

....

....

Day 121

*"Fear thou not; for I am with thee: **be not dismayed; for I am thy God: I will strengthen thee**; yea, I will help thee; yea, I will uphold thee with the right hand of my righteousness"* (Isaiah 41:10).

Greater is the Lord within me than any opposition or obstacle in the world.

May the presence and power of God lead, guide, and strengthen me for greater works. May this strength energize me to share God's unconditional love with others. May this same strength be perfected in all my weaknesses. May my words and actions bless the lives of those I encounter. I pray that the disappointments of the past will never reoccur in my life. In Jesus' name, amen.

Personal Prayers Journal

....

....

....

....

....

....

Day 122

*"Fear thou not; for I am with thee: be not dismayed; for I am thy God: I will strengthen thee; **yea, I will help thee; yea, I will uphold thee with the right hand of my righteousness**"* (Isaiah 41:10).

God is always faithful to His promises, and anyone who receives help from God will never fail in life but will continue to achieve success.

I pray that the Lord will assist me in all my endeavors and bring to fruition everything I set out to do. May I be empowered to overcome all obstacles. May failure be far from me. May His righteous hand guide me and bring me favor. May I be blessed with abundance and find favor in every aspect of my life. May those who are meant to support my destiny align themselves with me and show me great kindness as I embark on my journey today, in Jesus' Name, AMEN.

Personal Prayers Journal

....

....

....

....

Day 123

"This I say then, Walk in the Spirit, and ye shall not fulfil the lust of the flesh" (Galatians 5:16).

Walking is the act of moving from a stationary position towards a specific goal or purpose.

As I take my first steps today, I trust that God will guide me. I will not wander aimlessly or find myself in troublesome situations. I choose not to give in to my fleshly desires, and I refuse to let sin have control over me. With God's help, I will walk confidently and with purpose, both in the physical and spiritual realms, as I seek to fulfill God's promises for my life today. I pray all of this in Jesus' name, AMEN.

Personal Prayers Journal

....

....

....

....

....

....

....

Day 124

"The Lord is my strength and song, and is become my salvation" (Psalms 118:14).

A partnership with Christ assures us of His strength in our areas of weakness and guarantees success instead of failure.

May the Lord be merciful to me and forgive all of my sins today. May He be gracious unto me as He draws me closer in an intimate fellowship and relationship. May I receive strength for every weakness, and may songs of rejoicing fill my lips from today, in Jesus' Name, AMEN.

Personal Prayers Journal

....

....

....

....

....

....

....

....

....

Day 125

"So shalt thou find favour and good understanding in the sight of God and man" (Proverbs 3:4).

Favor is a fragrance that can unlock opportunities for supernatural promotion, increase, and expansion without requiring physical exertion.

Today, as I venture forth, I am confident that I will not face rejection, dejection, or denial. I will be enveloped in the sweet scent and essence of favor. The Lord will personally select me for His glory and greatness. Nations will eagerly extend their favor towards me, and individuals will arise to lend their support as I ascend to my position of visibility and influence. I declare this in the name of Jesus, AMEN.

Personal Prayers Journal

....

....

....

....

....

....

Day 126

"The righteous shall flourish like the cedar tree: He shall grow like a cedar in Lebanon" (Psalms 92:12).

As long as I continue to abide in the Lord, He helps me live a holy life and sustains me, just like the cedar tree known for its longevity.

Because I am the righteousness of God in Christ Jesus, I will fulfill the number of years allotted to me on earth in divine health and strength. I shall not become sick or be diagnosed with any terminal disease. My life will not be suddenly terminated or cut short. The Lord will add more years to my life. I will flourish in all seasons. I will no longer experience any dryness or drought for the rest of my days, today and always, in Jesus' Name. AMEN.

Personal Prayers Journal

....

....

....

....

....

....

Day 127

*"The righteous shall flourish like the cedar tree: **He shall grow like a cedar in Lebanon**" (Psalms 92:12).*

When I walk in obedience to God, I continue to grow in stature and wisdom, much like the cedar tree known for its longitudinal growth that allows it to stand out among other trees.

May I stand out and excel as I experience exponential growth. May my growth be multiplied. May I enter into a season of prominence and relevance as I rise above others starting today. May my growth not be hindered or limited. May I soar higher and break through into my greatness starting today, in Jesus' Name, AMEN.

Personal Prayers Journal

....

....

....

....

....

....

Day 128

"And the Spirit of the LORD will come upon thee, and thou shalt prophesy with them, and shalt be turned into another man" (1 Samuel 10:6).

The Holy Spirit is the comforter and our guide. Encountering the Holy Spirit is a life-changing and transformative experience.

May the Spirit of God rest powerfully upon me, and may my life never be the same again starting today. May my transformation be evident to all, as the Spirit of God fills me with continuous joy and jubilation every day. May my intimate fellowship with Him flourish daily, and may His presence always remain strong and never fade away. May I never grieve or lose His presence, but instead, may I have a lifelong relationship with Him as I journey into new horizons with the help of the Holy Spirit, starting today. In Jesus' name, AMEN.

Personal Prayers Journal

....

....

....

Day 129

*"And the Spirit of the LORD will come upon thee, **and thou shalt prophesy with them**, and shalt be turned into another man" (1 Samuel 10:6).*

A Prophecy is a divine revelation of God's heart and mind to Man. Only a few, by grace, are privileged to operate in the supernatural act of prophecy.

May the Lord count me worthy to be a vessel that reveals His heart. May my heart, ears, and eyes receive deep secrets from the Father. May I speak forth His word with precision and accuracy. I prophesy my greatness into reality, and may people be drawn to the brightness of my rising today, in Jesus' Name, AMEN.

Personal Prayers Journal

....

....

....

....

....

....

Day 130

*"And the Spirit of the LORD will come upon thee, and thou shalt prophesy with them, **and shalt be turned into another man**" (1 Samuel 10:6).*

The changes I experience after salvation are my spiritual transformation into His likeness. God transforms an ordinary person into an anointed vessel through His prophetic word.

———————————————

May my spiritual transformation be evident to all from today. May my past not affect my present. May my destiny helpers be activated today. May all past and present prophecies become a reality as I step out today, in Jesus' Name, AMEN.

Personal Prayers Journal

....

....

....

....

....

....

....

....

Day 131

"But I am like a green olive tree in the house of God: I trust in the mercy of God for ever and ever" (Psalms 52:8).

An olive tree is recognized by its beautiful green luster. I flourish and thrive when I remain connected to the true vine.

May my glory not be obscured. May the radiance and splendor of God's mighty hands on me be visible to all today. As I stay connected to the source of life daily, may I move from obscurity to prominence. In Jesus' Name, Amen.

Personal Prayers Journal

....

....

....

....

....

....

....

....

....

Day 132

*"And be not drunk with wine, wherein is excess; **but be filled with the Spirit**" (Ephesians 5:18).*

There are various types of spirits, but the spirit of God within me expels any opposing negative spirit.

May I be filled with the right Spirit - the Holy Spirit. May my body refuse any negetive spirits. May my body be open to the Spirit of truth. May the spirit of God distinguish me as a source of light and make me a threat to every ruler of darkness or any unfamiliar spirits today, in the name of Jesus, AMEN.

Personal Prayers Journal

....

....

....

....

....

....

....

Day 133

*"But I am like a green olive tree in the house of God: **I trust in the mercy of God for ever and ever**" (Psalms 52:8).*

God's divine mercy erases my transgressions and removes condemnation, shame, or guilt.

May God's mercy find me. May His mercy increase and bring favor into my life. May the spiritual cloak of mercy envelop me completely. May mercy eliminate any torment or accusations of sin, shame, or guilt from my life today, in Jesus' Name, AMEN.

Personal Prayers Journal

....

....

....

....

....

....

....

....

....

Day 134

*"**And be not drunk with wine, wherein is excess**; but be filled with the Spirit" (Ephesians 5:18).*

The infilling of the Holy Spirit is a lifelong experience of being intoxicated with God's constant presence, rather than being intoxicated with wine.

May I acknowledge God's life-giving word today. May I be filled with the Spirit of obedience that leads to a life of abundance. May I receive the rewards of obedience. May any unfamiliar spirits be exposed and driven away from me in seven different directions, as I walk in complete obedience from this day forward, in Jesus' Name, AMEN.

Personal Prayers Journal

....

....

....

....

....

....

....

Day 135

*"He will keep the feet of his saints, and the wicked shall be silent in darkness; **for by strength shall no man prevail**"*
(1 Samuel 2:9).

The arm of flesh will fail, but those who trust in God are never weary because He carries me with His everlasting arms.

———————————

May the Lord strengthen and sustain me. May His everlasting arms envelop and shield me from harm, and may His strong arms carry me through the storms of life to His divine rest and safety daily, in Jesus' Name, AMEN.

Personal Prayers Journal

....

....

....

....

....

....

....

....

....

Day 136

*"**After that thou shalt come to the hill of God**, where is the garrison of the Philistines: and it shall come to pass, when thou art come thither to the city, that thou shalt meet a company of prophets coming down from the high place with a psaltery, and a tabret, and a pipe, and a harp, before them; and they shall prophesy" (1Samuel 10:5).*

The Hill of God is a sacred site where people experience divine encounters, visitations, and find refuge. Those who ascend to the hill return with great joy.

I pray that the Lord will visit me in this place of prayer. May I have a personal encounter with Him and find safety in His presence. I also pray for permanent solutions to all the unresolved matters in my life today, in the name of Jesus. Amen.

Personal Prayers Journal

....

....

....

....

....

Day 137

"Then answered one of the servants, and said,
Behold, I have seen a son of Jesse the Bethlehemite"
(1 Samuel 16:18).

When the Lord lifts you up, others will also share your testimony, just like how David's testimony and success story were shared by another person in his absence.

May my name be remembered as the sole solution for a generational need. May the Spirit of God elevate me to a place of prominence. May I receive divine revelation and resources for success. May my story of greatness become a testimony that others share on my behalf today, in Jesus' name, AMEN.

Personal Prayers Journal

....
....
....
....
....
....

Day 138

"Behold, they shall surely gather together, but not by me:
whosoever shall gather together against thee shall fall for thy
sake" (Isaiah 54:15).

The presence of God is not found among those who seek to destroy destiny, but the devil never stops attacking God's chosen ones.

Since I am a covenant child of God, the Spirit of God will rise up to rebuke and torment any negative gathering that comes against me. May any voice that tries to distract me and any enemy of progress be silenced forever. May their language and voices be confused, just like the Tower of Babel, and may they be put to shame as I continue to rise higher from this day forward, in the name of Jesus, AMEN.

Personal Prayers Journal

....

....

....

....

....

Day 139

"Behold, they shall surely gather together, but not by me: ***whosoever shall gather together against thee shall fall for*** ***thy sake"*** *(Isaiah 54:15).*

The Lord is jealous and protective of all His children, so I ensure that I am counted as one of His beloved every day.

As I walk blamelessly before Him today, may the Angel of the Lord's goodness and mercy be my protector from the front and the rear. May anyone who tries to come against me be scattered. May any hand that is raised in judgment against me be plagued with leprosy. May all the ten plagues that plagued the relentless Egyptians and more befall my troublers if they refuse to repent today, in Jesus' Name, AMEN.

Personal Prayers Journal

....

....

....

....

....

....

Day 140

"The steps of a good man are ordered by the LORD: and he delighteth in his way" (Psalms37:23).

The confidence I have in living a righteous life keeps me in a right standing and relationship with God, allowing Him to lead, guide, and direct me.

———————————————

May the work of my hands speak for me in the throne room of Grace today. I trust that my steps will be ordered by God, and I will not unknowingly walk into any traps that are set to destroy or derail me. I rely on the Holy Spirit to be my guide from both the front and the rear. His double grace will be more than enough for me today, in Jesus' Name, AMEN.

Personal Prayers Journal

....

....

....

....

....

....

....

Day 147

"Then the king asked, "What is it, Queen Esther? What is your request?" (Esther 5:3).

Having complete trust in God and His unfailing favor has the power to nullify and override any laws, regulations, or rules established by human beings.

As I step out today, kings and nobles will be ready to assist me. The hand of God will intervene in my situation, bringing about a positive change. I am granted the grace to effortlessly make significant progress beyond what I can even imagine, starting from today. In Jesus' name, AMEN.

Personal Prayers Journal

....

....

....

....

....

....

....

....

Day 142

"Now when Joshua was near Jericho, he looked up and saw a man" (Joshua 5:13).

Spiritual sensitivity and discernment is a special gift from God that allows the audience to be in His presence at all times.

May my spiritual antenna be tuned to the right frequency to discern angelic visitations. May I receive the portion of my inheritance that is meant for me. May I step into the actualization and fulfillment of God's prophecy for my life today, in Jesus' Name, AMEN.

Personal Prayers Journal

....

....

....

....

....

....

....

....

Day 143

"Therefore thy gates shall be open continually; they shall not be shut day nor night; that men may bring unto thee the forces of the Gentiles, and that their kings may be brought" (Isaiah 60:11).

The blessings of a father showered upon a loving and obedient child cannot be taken away by anyone.

As I step out today, may I confidently move from obscurity to prominence, from disgrace to double grace, from distress to strength, from darkness to light, from striving to thriving, from stagnancy to soaring, from poverty to flourishing, from sickness to divine health. May my rise to the top be sudden and permanent, in Jesus' Name, AMEN.

Personal Prayers Journal

....

....

....

....

....

....

Day 144

"But ye shall receive power, after that the Holy Ghost is come upon you: and ye shall be witnesses unto me both in Jerusalem, and in all Judaea, and in Samaria, and unto the uttermost part of the earth" (Acts 1:8).

God is the only source of ultimate power, and as His child, He grants me the authority to operate and take control over any opposing forces of darkness.

May the power of the Holy Ghost rest upon me today. May all false and negative forces of darkness be expelled from my life. May the power of the Almighty God open doors of great opportunity and effectiveness for me. May this power also accelerate my progress towards success and eliminate any hindrances or delays today, in Jesus' Name, AMEN.

Personal Prayers Journal

....

....

....

....

....

....

Day 145

*"**For I will pour water upon him that is thirsty**, and floods upon the dry ground: I will pour my spirit upon thy seed, and my blessing upon thine offspring"* (Isaiah 44:3).

Physical and spiritual thirst can only be quenched with the water from the Fountain of Life, which is Christ Jesus.

May my thirsty soul be quenched by the spring of Living Water. May the spiritual deposit of fresh waters break up every fallow and dry ground, and may my barren land blossom into a fruitful vine filled with an abundance of delectable fruits that pertain to life today, in Jesus' Name, AMEN.

Personal Prayers Journal

....

....

....

....

....

....

....

....

Day 146

*"For I will pour water upon him that is thirsty, **and floods upon the dry ground**: I will pour my spirit upon thy seed, and my blessing upon thine offspring" (Isaiah 44:3).*

The infilling of the Holy Spirit is a promise from God for any soul that is dry and thirsty. The more I thirst for Him, the more I am filled and refreshed.

May I experience the filling of the Spirit of life every day. May this same spirit overflow and reverse any season of dryness or drought. May the spirit of His presence guide my steps, and may it manifest the fullness of His favor and the fulfillment of divine fellowship today, in Jesus' name, AMEN.

Personal Prayers Journal

....

....

....

....

....

....

....

Day 147

*"For I will pour water upon him that is thirsty, and floods upon the dry ground: **I will pour my spirit upon thy seed**, and my blessing upon thine offspring" (Isaiah 44:3).*

God is faithful to answer all of my petitions as I come to Him, fulfilling His promise to do so and even more for me and future generations.

May my empty vessel be filled with the Holy Spirit and power today. May the outpouring of this same Spirit flow unto my descendants for a thousand generations. From this day forward, my descendants will know, serve, and be eternally connected to the Lord Jesus Christ, in Jesus' Name, AMEN.

Personal Prayers Journal

....

....

....

....

....

....

....

Day 148

"And they shall spring up as among the grass, as willows by the water courses" (Isaiah 44:4).

Spring is a season of refreshment and blossoming that follows the dry season. It is accompanied by a burst of new life and energy.

I pray that I may embrace the newness of God's promises. May my hopes, good dreams, and glorious expectations fully manifest and bring about testimonies. May every experience of dryness and drought be replaced with a blossoming of blessings and freshness today, in Jesus' Name, AMEN.

Personal Prayers Journal

....

....

....

....

....

....

....

....

Day 149

*"For I will pour water upon him that is thirsty, and floods upon the dry ground: I will pour my spirit upon thy seed, **and my blessing upon thine offspring**" (Isaiah 44:3).*

God's blessings are an eternal covenant that He faithfully upholds, even when men fail to fulfill their end of the covenant.

May my blessings extend beyond my generation. May my descendants never experience a period of scarcity or separation from God, as we remain faithful to His covenant. Today, I proclaim and establish a lifelong connection with the One who multiplies blessings and elevates destinies. I step into a season of abundant blessings, and limitless opportunities, in Jesus' Name, AMEN.

Personal Prayers Journal

....

....

....

....

....

....

Day 150

"The LORD said unto my Lord, Sit thou at my right hand, until I make thine enemies thy footstool"
(Psalms 110:1).

The seat at God's right hand is reserved to honor His faithful and obedient children who qualify by virtue of their intimate relationship with Him.

———————————

May I be divinely and strategically placed in the seat of honor and power. May I occupy my seat of honor and dignity effortlessly. My seat will not be left empty, traded, or given to someone else. The Lord will guide me to that seat of great power, prominence, and prestige as I embark on my journey today, in Jesus' name. AMEN.

Personal Prayers Journal

....

....

....

....

....

....

Day 151

"The LORD said unto my Lord, Sit thou at my right hand, ***until I make thine enemies thy footstool"*** *(Psalms 110:1).*

It is a win-win situation when I partner with God because my enemies become His enemies.

The Lord will make all of my enemies bow before me as I continue to grow and achieve great heights. Those who persist in plotting my downfall will be beneath me, as I remain calm and composed. Unless they repent, they will be engulfed and buried in life's challenges. I will consistently overcome any schemes aimed at my downfall today, in Jesus' Name, AMEN.

Personal Prayers Journal

....

....

....

....

....

....

....

....

Day 152

"I had fainted, unless I had believed to see the goodness of the Lord in the land of the living" (Psalms 27:13).

God's goodness is always present in everything around me, as He is the creator and embodiment of all things good.

———————————

May the Lord enable me to see His goodness every day. May I never witness evil with my eyes, and may my ears be shielded from any negative reports or news that bring sorrow. I will only hear stories of joyful celebrations. May God's glory and goodness pave the way for me today and always, in the name of Jesus, AMEN.

Personal Prayers Journal

....

....

....

....

....

....

....

....

Day 153

*"**And it shall come to pass in the day** that the LORD shall give thee rest from thy sorrow, and from thy fear, and from the hard bondage wherein thou wast made to serve" (Isaiah 14:3).*

There is a designated day and time for everything, and it all started with the day and time when I found salvation and fully surrendered myself to Christ.

_____

May today be the designated day for the Lord to hear and answer all of my prayers. May all the pending requests I have turn into testimonies on this day. May today be a day of accountability and justice for all those who oppose me, in Jesus' Name, AMEN.

Personal Prayers Journal

....

....

....

....

....

....

Day 154

*"And it shall come to pass in the day that **the LORD shall give thee rest from thy sorrow, and from thy fear,** and from the hard bondage wherein thou wast made to serve"*
(Isaiah 14:3).

God is the only one who secures and watches over all His children. He replaces my paralyzing fear with His perfect faith.

May the Lord fill my mouth with praise reports instead of sorrow. May I dwell in the restful and loving arms of the Almighty. May all torments of fear be replaced with the perfection and comfort of the Holy Spirit today, in Jesus' Name. Amen.

Personal Prayers Journal

....

....

....

....

....

....

Day 155

*"And it shall come to pass in the day that **the LORD shall give thee rest** from thy sorrow, and from thy fear, **and from the hard bondage wherein thou wast made to serve***" (Isaiah 14:3).

There is rest for a child of God who trusts in God in the midst of the storm. Faith in God removes fear and delivers from bondage.

———————————

May any physical or spiritual chains, shackles that have held me stagnant be broken today. I am set free from oppression, suppression, depression, frustration, and any limitations today. I have broken free from any snares, and my soul, mind, body, and spirit shall dwell in God's rest and safety from today, in Jesus' Name, AMEN.

Personal Prayers Journal

....

....

....

....

....

....

Day 156

"Thus saith the Lord God, It shall not stand, neither shall it come to pass" (Isaiah 7:7).

No other voice is permitted to speak negativity into my life once God has proclaimed His blessings upon me.

God will silence and overpower every voice that speaks against my success with a spirit that cannot hear or speak. I will live in peace. May any malicious plans or meetings held against me be dispersed. May any harmful declarations be drowned out by God's thunderous voice, like the crashing of cymbals, as it surrounds me. Every negative word will be silenced and will not come to fruition today, in Jesus' name, AMEN.

Personal Prayers Journal

....

....

....

....

....

....

Day 157

"The whole earth is at rest, and is quiet: they break forth into singing" (Isaiah 14:7).

The Lord is the only one who can provide complete rest, even in the midst of turmoil, and He causes me to sing of His goodness in my life.

The Lord will quiet and calm my spirit. I will enjoy and experience divine rest when I go out and when I come in. I will have no reason to lament but instead wake up with songs of joy and victory daily, in Jesus' Name. Amen.

Personal Prayers Journal

....
....
....
....
....
....
....
....
....

Day 158

"And their seed shall be known among the Gentiles,
and their offspring among the people: all that see them shall
acknowledge them, that they are the seed which the LORD
hath blessed" (Isaiah 61:9).

The Light of God within me shines brightly, pulling me out of obscurity and illuminating my path, making me visible to all those who can help me fulfill my destiny.

May the light and glory of God upon my children be evident to all, guiding them towards greatness. My children will not remain hidden or pushed to the sidelines. They will be recognized for their remarkable accomplishments and extraordinary endeavors. From this day forward, their presence will strike fear into the hearts of both their known and unknown adversaries. In the powerful name of Jesus, I say amen.

Personal Prayers Journal

....

....

....

....

Day 159

*"And their seed shall be known among the Gentiles, and **thy offspring among the people**: all that see them shall acknowledge them, that they are the seed which the LORD hath blessed" (Isaiah 61:9).*

A seed that serves God creates a legacy of generational blessings by providing access to the key that unlocks more blessings.

May my seed continue to experience the goodness and greatness of God daily for a thousand generations. May my offspring never go hungry daily. May their legacy be firmly established forever. May my seed dwell in the glorious presence of God all the days of their lives, and may their lineage never stray from the path of the Lord. In Jesus' name, AMEN.

Personal Prayers Journal

....

....

....

....

....

Day 160

*"And their seed shall be known among the Gentiles, and their offspring among the people: **all that see them shall acknowledge them**, that they are the seed which the LORD hath blessed" (Isaiah 61:9).*

The Glory of God brings honor, recognition, dignity, and favor. It captures attention wherever I go.

May my light always shine brightly. May its radiance never diminish or be extinguished. May no darkness or spiritual blackout come upon me or my descendants. No evil eyes will gaze upon me or my offspring. People will be drawn to the brilliance of my glory. The Lord will declare my children as a blessing for generations to come, in Jesus' Name, AMEN.

Personal Prayers Journal

....

....

....

....

....

Day 161

*"And their seed shall be known among the Gentiles, and their offspring among the people: all that see them shall acknowledge them, **that they are the seed which the LORD hath blessed**" (Isaiah 61:9).*

God's glory and presence in my life will make me a visible manifestation of His blessings to the world.

The Lord will draw people's attention to me, as they are attracted to the radiance of His glory. My success will continue to shine, and my light will never fade. The powerful hand of God will rest upon me, lifting me up both physically and spiritually, to a place of prominence today, in Jesus' Name, AMEN.

Personal Prayers Journal

....

....

....

....

....

....

Day 162

*"**I will greatly rejoice in the LORD**, my soul shall be joyful in my God; for he hath clothed me with the garments of salvation, he hath covered me with the robe of righteousness, as a bridegroom decketh himself with ornaments, and as a bride adorneth herself with her jewels" (Isaiah 61:10).*

The decision to rejoice in the Lord aligns my path for God's goodness and limitless blessings every day.

———————————————

May this choice to rejoice in Him reverse any unfavorable situations for my benefit today. May my pathway be filled with success, destiny helpers, individuals who bring value, those who advance my career, and bearers of good news. Let all of them rise up to assist me in fulfilling heaven's divine mandate for my upliftment today, in Jesus' Name, AMEN.

Personal Prayers Journal

....

....

....

....

....

....

Day 163

*"And be not drunk with wine, wherein is excess; **but be filled with the Spirit**" (Ephesians 5:18).*

The Holy Spirit was sent to the world to comfort and guide me. I must empty myself of sin and surrender to His leading.

As I step out today, may the Spirit of the Lord fill me to overflow. May the same Spirit quicken and energize me. No contrary spirit will torment or come near my dwelling. Every negative spirit will be chased out of their hiding places and driven out of my life. May I exhibit the abiding fruits of His love, joy, peace, long-suffering, gentleness, meekness, goodness, faith, and temperance from today, in Jesus' Name, AMEN.

Personal Prayers Journal

....

....

....

....

....

....

Day 164

*"I will greatly rejoice in the LORD, **my soul shall be joyful in my God**; for he hath clothed me with the garments of salvation, he hath covered me with the robe of righteousness, as a bridegroom decketh himself with ornaments, and as a bride adorneth herself with her jewels" (Isaiah 61:10).*

The Lord commands joy and blessings to abound in my heart as I rejoice in Him. His presence is not with a discontented and sinful soul.

———————————

May the Lord cause me to be joyful and make my joy abound, multiply, and overflow. My joy will not suddenly end or turn into sorrow. Those who steal joy will not find me or come near my dwelling. Songs of rejoicing will never depart from me today, in Jesus' name, AMEN.

Personal Prayers Journal

....

....

....

....

....

....

Day 165

*"I will greatly rejoice in the LORD, my soul shall be joyful in my God; **for he hath clothed me with the garments of salvation, he hath covered me with the robe of righteousness**, as a bridegroom decketh himself with ornaments, and as a bride adorneth herself with her jewels"*
(Isaiah 61:10).

God's cloth of righteousness is His glory that covers me and makes me untouchable by those who wish to harm me.

May the spirit of life and the power of God envelop me. May my enemies be unable to decipher the secret behind my success. May my robe of righteousness captivate and introduce me to the influential people. May God's unseen hand elevate me even further today, in Jesus' Name, AMEN.

Personal Prayers Journal

....

....

....

....

....

....

Day 166

"And he believed in the Lord; and he counted it to him for righteousness" (Genesis 15:6).

Complete trust in God enables Him to take charge of my life and helps me to understand His responses: Yes, No, or Wait.

Today, may I experience the full benefits of righteousness that come from surrendering all my worries and concerns to the Almighty. May all my efforts be fruitful, and may my unwavering trust be rewarded with answers to prayers and solutions to challenges that are beyond human understanding. In Jesus' name, Amen.

Personal Prayers Journal

....

....

....

....

....

....

....

....

Day 167

*"I will greatly rejoice in the LORD, my soul shall be joyful in my God; for he hath clothed me with the garments of salvation, he hath covered me with the robe of righteousness, **as a bridegroom decketh himself with ornaments, and as a bride adorneth herself with her jewels**" (Isaiah 61:10).*

Physical adornment and beauty may fade over time, but a life lived in Christ experiences eternal radiance and the beauty of God.

May the Lord enhance and enrich my life starting from today. May my inner beauty never fade as His powerful hands illuminate His glory and radiance within me. I will continuously be a living testament to His wonders as His light shines upon me, setting me apart from others today, in the name of Jesus, AMEN.

Personal Prayers Journal

....

....

....

....

....

Day 168

*"I will greatly rejoice in the LORD, my soul shall be joyful in my God; **for he hath clothed me with the garments of salvation**, he hath covered me with the robe of righteousness, as a bridegroom decketh himself with ornaments, and as a bride adorneth herself with her jewels" (Isaiah 61:10).*

When the Lord bestows His presence and glory upon someone, they become untouchable and unreachable by anyone.

May the Lord envelop me in His covering. May any garments of shame or reproach that I am currently wearing be completely consumed by fire today. My enemies will never witness my vulnerability. The garment of salvation will be worn by every member of my household. I am blessed with the abundance of the morning, noon, and evening. May the Lord bless me, protect me, and illuminate His glory upon me and my descendants today, in the name of Jesus. Amen.

Personal Prayers Journal

....

....

....

Day 169

"And so, from the day we heard, we have not ceased to pray for you that you may be filled with the knowledge of His will in all spiritual wisdom and understanding" (Colossians 1:9).

God uses men to bless those he favors. Praying for my friends is a significant way to demonstrate my love and devotion to them.

May altars of prayer be raised daily on my behalf before God. May men arise to petition heaven for my breakthrough, as they also rise to expedite and uplift me. May all answers to my prayers be received while I am still speaking today, in Jesus' Name, AMEN.

Personal Prayers Journal

....

....

....

....

....

....

Day 170

*"And so, from the day we heard, we have not ceased to pray for you **that you may be filled with the knowledge of His will in all spiritual wisdom and understanding"** (Colossians 1:9).*

God is the source of wisdom, and He is willing to grant me knowledge and understanding of His will when I seek Him.

I pray that God will reveal His heart to me generously, showering me with grace, love, knowledge, and wisdom. May my spirit align with the pursuit of knowledge through persistence, perseverance, and endurance. I ask that any hindrance from my flesh that prevents the accurate fulfillment of God's will in my life be eliminated today, in Jesus' Name. AMEN.

Personal Prayers Journal

....

....

....

....

....

....

Day 171

*"**And out of them shall proceed thanksgiving and the voice of them that make merry:** and I will multiply them, and they shall not be few; I will also glorify them, and they shall not be small"* (Jeremiah 30:19).

The shouts of acclamation, rejoicing, and testimonies of God's goodness are the lifestyle of His anointed.

May my mouth be filled with laughter, my heart with love, my hands full of riches, my mind with peace and joy, and my home be filled with His glorious presence today and always, in Jesus' Name, AMEN.

Personal Prayers Journal

....

....

....

....

....

....

....

....

Day 172

*"**It is the spirit that quickeneth**; the flesh profiteth nothing: the words that I speak unto you, they are spirit, and they are life" (John 6:63).*

The deep that calls to the deep in the life of a Spirit-filled child of God awakens and cannot remain dormant or silent.

May the Spirit of God guide, direct, and revive any inactive or stagnant gift within me. May my body be energized by the same Spirit to run, overtake, and reclaim everything the enemy has taken from me. May the same Spirit of God fill me to overflowing with the grace to persevere until I achieve my breakthrough today, in Jesus' Name, AMEN.

Personal Prayers Journal

....

....

....

....

....

....

....

Day 173

*"And out of them shall proceed thanksgiving and the voice of them that make merry: **and I will multiply them, and they shall not be few**; I will also glorify them, and they shall not be small"* *(Jeremiah 30:19).*

Exponential growth is the result of divine multiplication, which occurs when I share my salvation story with someone and the Holy Spirit draws them towards Him.

May my blessings multiply starting today. The Lord will ensure that I receive double for my trouble. I will never decrease, be scarce, or diminish. Instead, I will live in abundance, opulence, and plenty as the Lord fulfills His promise to make me and what belongs to me a blessing from this day forward. In Jesus' Name, AMEN.

Personal Prayers Journal

....

....

....

....

....

....

Day 174

*"And out of them shall proceed thanksgiving and the voice of them that make merry: and I will multiply them, and they shall not be few; **I will also glorify them, and they shall not be small"** (Jeremiah 30:19).*

The glory of God has the power to increase the value of something small, make a few things seem countless, and elevate me from from a lowly to a highest position.

May the radiance of God's glory shine through me. May it attract people to favor and elevate me. My life will serve as a testament to His abundance and grace each day. People will share my stories of faith across the globe. I will expand in every direction, never remaining small. My blessings will extend to future generations, in Jesus' Name, AMEN.

Personal Prayers Journal

....

....

....

....

....

Day 175

*"It is the spirit that quickeneth; **the flesh profiteth nothing:** the words that I speak unto you, they are spirit, and they are life" (John 6:63).*

A life guided by the Spirit of God conquers all carnal desires, such as lustful thoughts and the desire for worldly recognition.

May the Spirit of God be present in me, and may I have control over my fleshly desires and I will not be controlled by them. May my spiritual sensitivity be attuned to the guidance of the Holy Spirit. May the Spirit of God direct me and lead me to encounter those who will assist me in fulfilling my destiny today, in Jesus' Name, Amen.

Personal Prayers Journal

....

....

....

....

....

....

....

Day 176

*"It is the spirit that quickeneth; the flesh profiteth nothing: **the words that I speak unto you, they are spirit, and they are life**" (John 6:63).*

God's words are spirit and life that penetrate my flesh, resonating and awakening His spirit within me.

May the word of life fully manifest in my life. May the spirit bring the Word to life, transforming me and creating powerful testimonies today. May God's profound call touch the depths of my being. May I never lack God's word. May my spiritual connection and relationship with the Father firmly establish His words in my life today and always, in Jesus' name, Amen.

Personal Prayers Journal

....

....

....

....

....

....

Day 177

"I waited patiently for the Lord, and He inclined unto me, and heard my cry" (Psalms 40:1).

God's divine visitation does not follow our calendar. He hears all my cries and will respond promptly, ensuring that my testimony is clear.

Today, the Lord is focused on me because my season of waiting is over. He will reward my patience with numerous testimonies. I will not wait in vain. My days of waiting are over. May God attentively listen to me, providing answers to all my long-awaited requests and solutions to unresolved problems today, in Jesus' Name, AMEN.

Personal Prayers Journal

....

....

....

....

....

....

....

Day 178

"He brought me up also out of an horrible pit, out of the miry clay, and set my feet upon a rock, and established my goings" (Psalms 40:2).

My journey through the valley of a horrible pit and miry clay is temporary; the Lord will lead me out at the appointed time and guide me towards my desired goal.

May the hand of the Lord be upon me every day. He will rescue me from any dreadful situation; my destiny will not be buried. God will establish my every step. Today, my faith and trust in Him will be strengthened, in Jesus' Name, AMEN.

Personal Prayers Journal

....

....

....

....

....

....

....

....

Day 179

"And he hath put a new song in my mouth, even praise unto our God: many shall see it, and fear, and shall trust in the Lord" (Psalms 40:3).

A new song is a testament to something new, and there is always rejoicing among the victorious.

Today, the Lord will fill my mouth with new songs of victory and joy. My songs of joy will be infectious, attracting the heavenly host choir and the open heavens of God's glory, beauty, and splendor over me as I step out today. In Jesus' Name, AMEN.

Personal Prayers Journal

....

....

....

....

....

....

....

....

Day 180

"Blessed is that man that makes the Lord his trust, and respected not the proud, nor such as turn aside to lies"
(Psalms 40:4).

I am blessed and rewarded when I place my complete trust in God, who always causes me to triumph and flourish in all areas of my life.

May the Lord continue to bless me abundantly as I cling to Him with unwavering trust. May I find pride and deceit repulsive. May the blessings and rewards that come from wholeheartedly trusting in God extend to future generations. May all who encounter me today recognize that I am truly favored by the Lord. In Jesus' name, amen.

Personal Prayers Journal

....

....

....

....

....

....

Day 181

"He guards all his bone, not one of them is broken"
(Psalms 34:20).

The presence of the Holy Spirit within me serves as a guide.
Additionally, He places men in my life to provide unwavering
support and encouragement.

May I be surrounded daily by all the physical and spiritual
resources I require. Let individuals arise to fortify and uplift
me, and may my encouragers never turn their backs on me.
My source of strength will not diminish, and I will not be left
vulnerable or shattered. Today, may the Lord Himself serve as
my spiritual support and shield from any evil or misfortune,
in the powerful name of Jesus, AMEN.

Personal Prayers Journal

....

....

....

....

....

....

Day 182

"Be pleased, O Lord, to deliver me" (Psalms 40:13).

God is the ultimate deliverer from all types of trouble. He is always prompt to answer and save me when I call upon Him.

May my life be pleasing to the Father, the only one who can deliver me from any limitations or challenges I may face today. He will rescue me from every trouble on this earth and from all my problems. May He rise up and deliver me from both known and unknown battles. May He set me free from any kind of addiction and protect me with His loving arms throughout this day. In Jesus' Name, Amen.

Personal Prayers Journal

....

....

....

....

....

....

....

....

Day 183

"I sought the Lord, and He heard me" (Psalms 34:4)

Be intentional in seeking God by communicating with Him. When you seek God, you will find Him.

May the grace to seek God be released upon me today. May the God of Jacob hear and respond to all my requests as I seek Him. May the heavens over my head never be shut, in Jesus' Name, AMEN.

Personal Prayers Journal

....

....

....

....

....

....

....

....

....

....

Day 184

"Be pleased, O LORD, make haste to help me"
(Psalms 40:13).

God knows and hears the cries of His children; He sends angels in our time of need to assist me. As a child of God, I believe that my challenges will be met with divine timing.

———————————————

May my voice be acknowledged in both heaven and earth today. The Lord will promptly answer my prayers even before I finish speaking. May the blessings from our loving Father not be hindered, altered, postponed, or prevented. The Lord will swiftly come to my aid today, in Jesus' Name, AMEN.

Personal Prayers Journal

....

....

....

....

....

....

....

....

Day 185

"Let them be ashamed and confounded together that seek after my soul to destroy it" (Psalms 40:14).

God is jealous of all His children, including me. He thwarts any negative plans that may cause me harm.

May the Lord bring shame upon all my enemies. May the camp of my enemies be thrown into disarray and confusion when they hear my name mentioned. May the Lord scatter and annihilate anyone plotting evil against me, and may God remove from my path all those planning to waste my time today, in Jesus' name, Amen.

Personal Prayers Journal

....

....

....

....

....

....

....

....

Day 186

*"**He hath shewed thee, O man, what is good**; and what doth the LORD require of thee, but to do justly, and to love mercy, and to walk humbly with thy God?" (Micah 6:8).*

We serve a benevolent God who delights in demonstrating to me that the sole path to a life of abundance is through Him alone.

May the Lord illuminate the way for me to follow. My days will be filled with glad tidings. God will direct my footsteps solely towards the path of life. His presence will lead and guide me. I will witness and partake in all the blessings that God has in store for me in this life, and everything that is associated with goodness and godliness shall be my portion today, in the name of Jesus, amen.

Personal Prayers Journal

....

....

....

....

....

....

Day 187

*"He hath shewed thee, O man, what is good; **and what doth the LORD require of thee, but to do justly, and to love mercy, and to walk humbly with thy God?**" (Micah 6:8).*

God's expectations from all His children are never burdensome, neither are they meant to cause harm to anyone. His love for me is unconditional and eternal.

The word of God will come to pass in my life with utmost accuracy. May I receive the grace to stay away from anything that appears evil. May my heart be filled with mercy and grace as I strive to do what is necessary and walk uprightly before God from this day forward, in the name of Jesus, Amen.

Personal Prayers Journal

....

....

....

....

....

....

....

Day 188

"Let them be driven backward and put to shame that wish me evil" (Psalms 40:14).

Dwelling in the presence of God makes me a vessel of His light and power, and diminishes any attraction for those who do evil around me.

May all evil arrows be redirected to the sender, and may any evildoers who plot harm against me be left bewildered and confused. May the hearts, minds, and hands of all evildoers be rendered incapable of carrying out their wicked schemes against me. May my spirit, soul, and body repel every evil assault upon me through the power and mercy found in the precious blood of Jesus today, in Jesus' Name, AMEN.

Personal Prayers Journal

....

....

....

....

....

....

Day 189

"Let them be desolate for a reward of their shame that say unto me, Aha, aha" (Psalms 40:15)

God's goodness always prevails over the evil agendas of men. My silence towards naysayers gives God an opportunity to speak for me and prove them wrong.

———————————

May the Lord expose and shame all hidden secrets or negative agendas of my haters. May the Lord remove those friends who are enemies and enemies who pretend to be friends from my life. May anyone who seeks to destroy me in secret be openly disgraced and embarrassed. The Lord will arise on my behalf, rewarding me doubly for all my troubles today, in Jesus' name, AMEN.

Personal Prayers Journal

....

....

....

....

....

....

Day 190

*"**Let all those that seek thee rejoice and be glad in thee:** let such as love thy salvation say continually, The Lord be magnified" (Psalms 40:16).*

There is immense joy and boundless pleasure when I seek God daily. He takes pleasure in fellowshipping and spending time with me.

May I receive the grace to seek the Lord every day. May the heavens be opened to me as I join the twenty-four elders in worship. May rejoicing and gladness become daily experiences in my life starting today, in Jesus' Name, AMEN.

Personal Prayers Journal

....

....

....

....

....

....

....

....

Day 191

*"Let all those that seek thee rejoice and be glad in thee: **let such as love thy salvation say continually, The Lord be magnified**" (Psalms 40:16).*

The father's heart desires for everyone to be saved and come to know the Lord Jesus Christ.

May my life serve as a beacon that attracts people to the path of repentance and salvation. May my testimonies reflect the divine glory of God. May the grace to live a life of holiness and righteousness always keep me in His divine presence each day. In Jesus' Name, Amen.

Personal Prayers Journal

....

....

....

....

....

....

....

....

Day 192

"But I am poor and needy; yet the Lord thinks of me; thou art my help and my deliverer; do not delay, O my God" (Psalms 40:17).

God has a deep concern for the poor and the needy, as He bears full responsibility for their well-being and meeting all their needs.

I pray that the Lord will embrace me in His loving arms and protect me from any harm. May I always experience the goodness of God while I am alive. May any physical limitations of lack be reversed as I experience abundance and have more than enough always. May I also partake in the spiritual covenant that leads to eternal blessings. May I enjoy the rich blessings of His glory and the abundant life found in Christ from this day forward. In Jesus' name, amen.

Personal Prayers Journal

....

....

....

....

....

Day 193

*"But I am poor and needy; yet the Lord thinks of me; **thou art my help and my deliverer; do not delay, O my God"** (Psalms 40:17).*

God is always on time, never early or late. He is the ever-present help in times of need, ready to assist me at all times.

May my prayers receive instant answers, and may any delays be removed from your life. May the great Deliverer rise to help me today in everything I set out to do, in Jesus' Name, AMEN.

Personal Prayers Journal

....

....

....

....

....

....

....

....

....

Day 194

"Thus will I bless thee while I live: I will lift up my hands in thy name" (Psalms 63:4).

A heart that is overflowing with praise and thanksgiving opens the door to experience the divine presence and the glory of God.

_____

May the heart of the Father be pleased with me. May the Lord carry and sustain me as I lift up my voice in loving adoration. May God the Father, Son, and Holy Spirit acknowledge and bless me with multiple opportunities today in the name of Jesus. AMEN.

Personal Prayers Journal

....

....

....

....

....

....

....

....

Day 195

*"And I will make of thee a great nation, and **I will bless thee, and make thy name great; and thou shalt be a blessing"***
(Genesis 12:2).

God's words and promises are eternally established because He is faithful to fulfill them and carefully observes His word to bring it to pass.

May the Word of God be fully realized in my daily life. May I bear abundant fruit, increase, and bring blessings to the earth. May I never be disregarded or ignored as the Lord establishes my name for an everlasting covenant of blessings that impact both my life and future generations. May I effortlessly enter into seasons of open doors every day, in the name of Jesus. Amen.

Personal Prayers Journal

....
....
....
....
....
....

Day 196

"Happy is he that hath the God of Jacob for his help who's hope is in The Lord his God" (Psalms 146:5).

Having God as my ally and help brings me peace of mind because I know that He is capable of handling any challenges that come my way. The God I serve is always there to support me when I need it the most.

As I embark on each day this year, I trust that the God of Jacob will assist me. May He open doors of success for me, and may He never abandon me. I pray that my hope in Him will never be shattered. In Jesus' name, AMEN.

Personal Prayers Journal

....

....

....

....

....

....

....

....

Day 197

*"And the angel of the LORD appeared unto him, and said unto him, **The LORD is with thee, thou mighty man of valour**" (Judges 6:12).*

The Lord sees and ignites the greatness He has placed within all His children, even when I am filled with doubt about myself.

May God's power eradicate every trace of self-doubt and limitations within me. May His presence elevate and position me before influential figures, rather than ordinary individuals. May my glory never be concealed or suppressed, and may I make significant strides towards my breakthroughs and blessings today, in the Name of Jesus, AMEN.

Personal Prayers Journal

....
....
....
....
....
....

Day 198

"Thou hast enlarged my steps under me, that my feet did not slip" (Psalms 18:36).

The Lord is my spiritual guide who constantly holds my hand, leading and guiding me to ensure I do not get lost or miss my way.

May I increase physically, spiritually, and mentally. May I be firmly planted on the solid rock of Christ, and may my feet not slip, causing me to fall or fail. Lord, please make room for me to enlarge and expand in all areas of my life from this day forward, in Jesus' Name, AMEN.

Personal Prayers Journal

....

....

....

....

....

....

....

....

Day 199

"It is God that girdeth me with strength, and maketh my way perfect" (Psalms 18:32).

The strength and power of God is exhibited in all of His children who are willing to operate in faith.

May the Lord perfect His strength in all my weakness. May God show forth and show up for me. May the God of Abraham, Isaac, and Jacob carry me through the storms, fire, and winds of life to victory from today, in Jesus' Name, AMEN.

Personal Prayers Journal

....

....

....

....

....

....

....

....

Day 200

*"It is God that girdeth me with strength, **and maketh my way perfect**" (Psalms 18:32).*

My God is perfect and good. Therefore, I strive to walk towards perfection as I allow Him to purify me.

My path and journey with God will always be consistent. Every crooked path will be made straight. The Lord will serve as a lamp and guide to light my way, and all imperfections will be eliminated starting today, in Jesus' Name, AMEN.

Personal Prayers Journal

....

....

....

....

....

....

....

....

....

....

Day 201

*"**And the angel of the LORD appeared unto him**, and said unto him, The LORD is with thee, thou mighty man of valour"* (Judges 6:12)

An angelic visitation serves to affirm God's presence within me and alongside me, eradicating any fear I may have.

───────────────

May the Lord dispatch angels to carry out tasks on my behalf. May my divine encounter with Yahweh open all doors of restriction in my journey. May I experience eternal favor today, in Jesus' Name, AMEN.

Personal Prayers Journal

....

....

....

....

....

....

....

....

....

Day 202

"Thou hast also given me the shield of thy salvation: and thy right hand hath holden me up, and thy gentleness hath made me great" (Psalms 18:35).

The gift of salvation is the most powerful gift from God to all His children. It grants me direct access to God at all times.

———————————

May my relationship with Christ be strengthened daily. May the Lord reveal Himself to me more. May I have the privilege of ruling and reigning with Him eternally. May my crown of stars abound as I faithfully serve Him, in Jesus' name. AMEN.

Personal Prayers Journal

....

....

....

....

....

....

....

Day 203

*"Thou hast also given me the shield of thy salvation: **and thy right hand hath holden me up**, and thy gentleness hath made me great" (Psalms 18:35).*

The right hand of the Lord is mighty and powerful enough to sustain the entire earth and guide me through life's challenges and difficulties.

May the Lord support me with His righteous right hand. May my name be forever remembered and written in the palm of His hand. May the Lord carry me, protecting me from stumbling. His mighty and powerful hands will elevate me above my contemporaries, leading me to triumph today, in the name of Jesus, AMEN.

Personal Prayers Journal

....

....

....

....

....

....

Day 204

*"Thou hast also given me the shield of thy salvation: and thy right hand hath holden me up, **and thy gentleness hath made me great**" (Psalms 18:35).*

We serve a loving Father who treats us with unparalleled kindness and love, without any bias.

———————————————

May I experience His gentleness, joy, and peace every day starting from today. May His boundless love create a chain reaction of numerous opportunities for my personal growth, in Jesus' Name, AMEN.

Personal Prayers Journal

....

....

....

....

....

....

....

....

Day 205

*"**And Samuel lay until the morning, and opened the doors of the house of the LORD**. And Samuel feared to shew Eli the vision" (1 Samuel 3:15).*

The door to the house of the Lord is always open to those with willing and receptive hearts. When I open my heart, He comes to dwell inside and guide my ways.

May the doors of my heart always remain open to receive God's word and instruction daily. May the word of God continually do me good, and may doors of blessings be open for me each day. Today, I will not walk into doors of shame, sadness, sickness, or sorrow, in Jesus' Name, AMEN.

Personal Prayers Journal

....

....

....

....

....

....

....

Day 206

"And the LORD appeared unto him in the plains of Mamre: and he sat in the tent door in the heat of the day"
(Genesis 18:1).

The platform of angelic visitation is where divine encounters occur and extraordinary miracles take place.

———————————————

May the Lord visit me at my tent of miracles. May my encounter with angelic visitation result in the manifestation of my "ISAAC," symbolizing continuous laughter, fulfilled promises, and a new identity. Lord, please eliminate any reproach or barrenness from my life today, in Jesus' Name, AMEN.

Personal Prayers Journal

....

....

....

....

....

....

....

Day 207

"He who earnestly seeks righteousness and loyalty finds life, righteousness, and honor" (Proverbs 21:21).

Seeking God daily is the pathway to a life of holiness and righteousness. My loyalty and commitment are shown through constant daily fellowship.

As I seek and abide in the path of righteousness, may I enjoy all the blessings of being a child of God with honor and dignity. May my life's testimonies exhibit holiness, righteousness, loyalty, and dignity today, in Jesus' Name, AMEN.

Personal Prayers Journal

....

....

....

....

....

....

....

....

Day 208

"I will instruct thee and teach thee in the way which thou shalt go: I will guide thee with mine eye" (Psalms 32:8).

The greatest privilege for a child of God is to be in association with the best teacher, counselor, and instructor, who is the Lord Almighty.

———————————————

May I be granted the grace to receive and accept divine instructions today. May the all-seeing and all-powerful God guide and lead me on the right path. May I not lose my way as I enter into a life filled with divine health, joy, peace, favor, and breakthrough today, in the name of Jesus, AMEN.

Personal Prayers Journal

....

....

....

....

....

....

....

....

Day 209

*"I will instruct thee and teach thee in the way which thou shalt go: **I will guide thee with mine eye**" (Psalms 32:8).*

The eyes of God is all seeing more than anyone else. He is able to show me the invisible that is profitable when received by a willing and receptive heart.

———————————

May the grace to receive and run with the wise counsel from the Father be released to me. May the eyes of the Lord guide me and illuminate any darkness on my path. May the life transforming counsel hand of God bring to accurate physical manifestation of every fruit of the spirit as I step out today, in Jesus Name, AMEN.

Personal Prayers Journal

....

....

....

....

....

....

....

Day 210

"You who answer prayer, to you all people will come"
(Psalms 65:2).

There is an assurance for me that God will answer the prayers of all who come to Him with an expectation.

The Lord, who is the God of Abraham, Isaac, and Jacob, will answer me as I seek His face. I will not be disgraced or put to shame as I petition heaven. Today, in the place of prayer, I will experience positive and accelerated response. In Jesus' name, amen..

Personal Prayers Journal

....

....

....

....

....

....

....

....

Day 211

"And the sons of Carmi; Achar, the troubler of Israel, who transgressed in the thing accursed" (1 Chronicles 2:7).

The devil's plan is always to steal, kill, and destroy. However, God's power can overcome all of the devil's plans.

_____

I pray that every door of affliction, addiction, or violation over my life may be destroyed. I ask the Lord to reveal and expose anyone who troubles, frustrates, or tries to separate my helpers from my life. I also pray that any negative circle of frustration in my life may be broken. As I step out today, I pray that I may walk in complete victory in Jesus' name, AMEN.

Personal Prayers Journal

....

....

....

....

....

....

....

Day 212

"But when they were in their trouble and distress they turned to the LORD God of Israel. And in earnest desperation, he sought the Lord, and He let them find Him" (2 Chronicles 15:4).

I am grateful that God sees and hears me when I cry out to Him because He is the only one who can deliver me from any of my troubles and distress.

———————————————

May the Lord bring calm to my troubled soul today. May I find peace and joy as I seek and turn to the Lord. May I be lifted out of any state of distress, depression, or trouble as I dwell in the secret place of the Most High God. May the calm and comforting embrace of the Lord Jesus be with me throughout today, in Jesus' name, Amen.

Personal Prayers Journal

....

....

....

....

....

....

Day 213

*"But when they were in their trouble and distress they turned to the LORD God of Israel. **And in earnest desperation, he sought the Lord, and He let them find Him**"*
(2 Chronicles 15:4).

When you sincerely seek God, He reaches out to you because He sees and knows those whose hearts and minds are turned toward Him.

As I seek Him with complete surrender today, may the grace to persevere and abide in Him be released to me. May the Lord find me and show me mercy. May I receive solutions to all the desires of my heart in His presence today, in Jesus' Name, AMEN.

Personal Prayers Journal

....

....

....

....

....

....

Day 214

*"**Then Elisha said, Hear ye the word of the LORD**; Thus saith the LORD, To morrow about this time shall a measure of fine flour be sold for a shekel, and two measures of barley for a shekel, in the gate of Samaria" (2 Kings 7:1).*

God's word is quick, powerful, and sharper than any two-edged sword. It manifests and performs.

May my ears be opened to hear the word of life today. May the Word of Life bring life to my mortal body. May the word of God remove any dead situation, delay, or stagnancy around me. May heaven stand ready to support every word that comes from my mouth today, in Jesus' Name, AMEN.

Personal Prayers Journal

....

....

....

....

....

....

....

Day 215

"Then Elisha said, Hear ye the word of the LORD; **Thus saith the LORD, To morrow about this time shall a measure of fine flour be sold for a shekel,** *and two measures of barley for a shekel, in the gate of Samaria" (2 Kings 7:1).*

An unpleasant situation is instantly transformed into pleasantness when the glory of God's presence abides with His beloved.

May the Lord's presence be with me. May all past struggles become success stories as I step into my day. May the God of divine turnaround transform all negative situations and reports for my good. May the grace to achieve, succeed, and move forward with ease be released to me, in Jesus' Name, AMEN.

Personal Prayers Journal

....

....

....

....

....

....

Day 216

"Tell ye the daughter of Sion, Behold, thy King cometh unto thee, meek, and sitting upon an ass, and a colt the foal of an ass" (Matthew 21:5).

God's chronology is different from man's clock. A day of divine visitation can eliminate years of waiting.

May the King of kings remember me today. May God visit me with His divine presence and show up in my situation today. May the door and access to my new season be opened for me. May the on-time God, who is never late, grant all my desires and transform my trials into testimonies today, in Jesus' Name, AMEN.

Personal Prayers Journal

....

....

....

....

....

....

....

Day 217

*"Tell ye the daughter of Sion, Behold, thy King cometh unto thee, meek, **and sitting upon an ass, and a colt the foal of an ass**" (Matthew 21:5).*

God is adorned with both humility and splendor, virtues that can only be nurtured through the constant presence of God in our lives.

———————————

May the Lord's presence dwell within and uphold me each day. May the spirit of pride find no refuge in my life. Today, I pray for the grace to maintain gentleness and humility as I journey towards triumph, just as I ride on my triumphant colt. In Jesus' Name, AMEN.

Personal Prayers Journal

....

....

....

....

....

....

Day 218

"And the blind and the lame came to Him in the temple area, and He healed them" (Matthew 21:14).

The great physician, Jehovah Rapha, is ready to heal all those who come to Him. It requires me to take a step of faith in order to receive my healing.

————————————

May my path today be guided towards the divine presence of Jehovah Rapha. May every spirit of lameness or blindness be reversed. I receive healing and strength in every area of weakness today, in Jesus' name, AMEN.

Personal Prayers Journal

....

....

....

....

....

....

....

....

Day 219

"When Jesus had received the sour wine, He said, It is finished!" (John 19:30).

The Lord has the ultimate authority over my life and my current situations and circumstances, regardless of what others may say.

———————————

May all sorrow, sadness, sinful tendencies, and sickness be removed and replaced with a spirit of praise. From this day forward, may I rise up and walk in victory over any past frustrations. May the negative chapters of my life be transformed into positive ones. May those who previously said no to me now call me back with a yes, and may those who rejected me before now accept me. In Jesus' name, AMEN.

Personal Prayers Journal

....

....

....

....

....

Day 220

"Casting all your care upon Him for He cares for you"
(1 Peter 5:7).

The only person who is never tired of listening to and taking care of one's concerns, heart-cry, and burdens is the Lord, Jesus.

———————————————

As I cast all my care on Jesus today, may He embrace and lift me up with His ever-loving arms. May He shield, sustain, and strengthen me. May all my burdens be lifted as I receive the garment of praise for every spirit of heaviness today, in Jesus' Name, AMEN.

Personal Prayers Journal

....
....
....
....
....
....
....
....

Day 221

*"Casting all your care upon Him **for He cares for you**"*
(1 Peter 5:7).

The Lord loves and cares for all His children. His promise is to care for those who cast all their cares on Him.

———————————

As I identify, trust, and surrender to the authority of Christ, may His angels of goodness and mercy follow me. May I receive the grace to overcome impossible challenges and achieve the unimaginable. May I have the grace to reach all my life goals in this season. May my small efforts attract abundance today, in Jesus' Name, AMEN.

Personal Prayers Journal

....

....

....

....

....

....

....

....

Day 222

*"**And it came to pass, that while they communed together and reasoned,** Jesus himself drew near, and went with them"*
(Luke 24:15).

When Jesus journeys with me, there is a shift from struggling situations to successful accomplishments.

———————————————

May all the desires of my heart assuredly come to pass as Jesus steps into my life and current situation today. May all the testimonies I have been waiting for, miracles, and open doors become showers of answered prayers today. May the spirit of delay be permanently erased. May every struggle be replaced with the timely arrival of my blessings. In Jesus' name, amen.

Personal Prayers Journal

....

....

....

....

....

....

Day 223

*"And it came to pass, that while they communed together and reasoned, **Jesus himself drew near, and went with them**"*
(Luke 24:15).

The presence and power of the Lord are with any gathering of His saints. All I need to do is invite Him in.

───────────────

As I commune in the presence of Jehovah, may He draw near to me. May the Lord go ahead and abide with me, manifesting His glory and presence in my life today. May I receive the wisdom to petition and reason with clarity. May confusion never befall me. May the Father give me urgent and timely attention. Today, I experience divine visitation and the manifestation of miracles, signs, and wonders, in Jesus' Name. AMEN.

Personal Prayers Journal

....

....

....

....

....

....

Day 224

"But we trusted that it had been he which should have redeemed Israel: and beside all this, today is the third day since these things were done" (Luke 24:21).

The significance of the Lord's resurrection on the third day is that He exchanged the key of death for the key of life.

Today, I declare that I will rise above any form of physical, spiritual, emotional, or mental struggle. I will also overcome any financial hardships, stagnancy, delays, spiritual confinement, or imprisonment. I am liberated and set free from the enemy's hold over my life. Today, I will rise to my rightful place of success and prominence, in Jesus' name. AMEN.

Personal Prayers Journal

....
....
....
....
....
....

Day 225

"And their eyes were opened, and they knew him; and he vanished out of their sight" (Luke 24:31).

My close relationship with God allows me to see beyond the physical realm. It reveals that nothing is more limiting than having eyes but lacking both physical and spiritual sight.

———————————————

From this day forward, I am free from any stigma of physical or spiritual blindness. May every barrier that has hindered my vision, preventing me from seeing the King of kings, be removed today. May my eyes only behold the goodness and glory of God from now on. May I discern the direct path to my opportunities for greatness every day. Therefore, my vision will not be clouded, hindered, isolated, or obscured anymore, starting today, in Jesus' Name, AMEN.

Personal Prayers Journal

....

....

....

....

....

....

....

Day 226

"and hope does not put us to shame, because God's love has been poured into our hearts through the Holy Spirit who has been given to us" (Romans 5:5).

God is love. His love for us is eternal and unbiased, unconditional, and forgiving, without any shame or condemnation.

May I experience the abundant outpouring of God's love today. May His loving arms envelop me as He warms my heart with His love. May that same love sustain and carry me through any difficulty or storms of life as He lovingly sings and rejoices over me today, in Jesus' name. Amen.

Personal Prayers Journal

....

....

....

....

....

....

....

Day 227

"For the LORD had caused the Aramean army to hear the sound of chariots, and the sound of horses, the sound of a great army" (2 Kings 7:6).

Our Lord Jesus Christ is described as the mighty man of war who rises on my behalf to defeat all my enemies.

May my enemies be completely bewildered as they hear the sound of the Lord's powerful army. May the Spirit of God establish a strong defense against any gathering that opposes my progress. May my steps be greatly amplified as I step out with Jehovah Sabbaoth today, in Jesus' name, AMEN.

Personal Prayers Journal

....

....

....

....

....

....

....

....

Day 228

"Then they said one to another, We do not well: this day is a day of good tidings, and we hold our peace: if we tarry till the morning light, some mischief will come upon us: now, therefore, come, that we may go and tell the king's household"
(2 Kings 7:9).

I have received good news because of my relationship and divine connection with God.

May my destiny be intertwined with individuals who can be trusted with the treasures of hidden places. May I always be a messenger and bringer of good news. May I have unfettered access to influential people in high positions as I share good news with others. May my voice be sought after and preferred by leaders all over the world. May I speak daily about the good news of salvation to my generation and beyond, in Jesus' Name, AMEN.

Personal Prayers Journal

....

....

....

....

Day 229

*"**Then shalt thou go on forward from thence**, and thou shalt come to the plain of Tabor, and there shall meet thee three men going up to God to Bethel, one carrying three kids, and another carrying three loaves of bread, and another carrying a bottle of wine" (1 Samuel 10:3).*

God expects all His children to make progress and advance in life. His plan for me does not include stagnation or regression.

Today, I pray that every spirit of stagnation is eliminated from my life. I am determined to keep moving forward and making strides in life. I refuse to settle for a mediocre existence. I ask the Lord to permanently close the doors of limitations, redundancy, and stagnation, while opening doors of advancement, promotion, and elevation for me. May I be filled with the grace and determination to pursue and achieve all of God's plans and purposes for my life, in Jesus' name, AMEN.

Personal Prayers Journal

....

....

Day 230

*"Then shalt thou go on forward from thence, **and thou shalt come to the plain of Tabor**, and there shall meet thee three men going up to God to Bethel, one carrying three kids, and another carrying three loaves of bread, and another carrying a bottle of wine"* (1 Samuel 10:3).

The plain of Tabor holds great significance as it is a place where divine encounters occur, including the transfiguration of our Lord.

I pray that I may swiftly reach my place of favor and rest. May the Lord be with me, guiding and transforming my destiny for the better. As I step into the place where divine favor awaits me today, may I be transformed into a new person. May I not lose my way or get distracted on my journey to the plain of Tabor (the place of divine encounter) today. In Jesus' name, AMEN.

Personal Prayers Journal

....

....

....

....

Day 231

*"Then shalt thou go on forward from thence, and thou shalt come to the plain of Tabor, **and there shall meet thee three men going up to God to Bethel, one carrying three kids, and another carrying three loaves of bread, and another carrying a bottle of wine**" (1 Samuel 10:3).*

I surrender to God, who knows and orchestrates each day. He will lead me to Bethel, the place of divine blessings.

———————————————

May the Lord order my steps to the place of divine visitation. May the Trinity - God the Father, Son, and Holy Spirit - show up at my Bethel, bearing life-sustaining gifts of abundance, fruitfulness, and complete wholeness in my health today and always. In Jesus' Name, AMEN.

Personal Prayers Journal

....

....

....

....

....

....

Day 232

"Blessed are the merciful: for they shall obtain mercy"
(Matthew 5:7).

I serve a God who is abundantly merciful every day. Falling into His hands when I make mistakes is far more preferable than facing ruthless enemies.

———————————

As I begin my day, I pray that God's mercy will speak on my behalf, guarding and guiding my every step. I will not be lost or wander aimlessly through life's endless cycles. May God's compassion and mercy lead me to the door of my miracles. Starting today, may mercy elevate me to the place of my blessings. In Jesus' name, AMEN.

Personal Prayers Journal

....

....

....

....

....

....

Day 233

*"**And Jesus went forth, and saw a great multitude, and was moved with compassion toward them,** and He healed the sick" (Matthew 14: 14).*

A heart of compassion is not common among men, but I serve a God who is compassionate and abundant in mercy and grace.

――――――――――――――

May the Lord be gracious and compassionate towards me. May my sins not stand against me on the day of my blessing. Let mercy open the doors to miracles for me and provide supernatural help daily as I show compassion to others, in Jesus' Name, AMEN.

Personal Prayers Journal

....

....

....

....

....

....

....

Day 234

*"And Jesus went forth, and saw a great multitude, and was moved with compassion toward them, **and He healed their sick**" (Matthew 14: 14).*

Healing is the nourishment for all of God's children, accessible through His goodness, compassion, love, and mercy.

———————————————

May the healing power of the Lord flow and reverse any kind of illness in my body today. Let the Lord remove any physical, emotional, mental, and spiritual affliction that has caused any hindrance or stagnation in my life today, in Jesus' name, AMEN.

Personal Prayers Journal

....

....

....

....

....

....

....

Day 235

*"Brethren, I count not myself to have apprehended: **but this one thing I do, forgetting those things which are behind**, and reaching forth unto those things which are before"*
(Philippians 3: 13).

The journey to living a righteous and godly life involves making the decision to move on from negative past events.

May all unpleasant experiences from the past be erased and replaced with indescribable joy. May the Lord bring me daily blessings that fill my heart with joy. May He protect and direct my heart, shielding it from any previous regrets or distractions. May all traces of backsliding and limitations be eliminated, making way for a future filled with new opportunities for me today, in Jesus' Name, AMEN.

Personal Prayers Journal

....

....

....

....

....

....

Day 236

*"Brethren, I count not myself to have apprehended: but this one thing I do, forgetting those things which are behind, **and reaching forth unto those things which are before**" (Philippians 3: 13).*

The key to reaching milestones and progressing quickly is by concentrating on present and future objectives.

May the Lord keep my mind sharp, my spirit vibrant, and my heart fixed on the path to a fulfilling life. May I no longer face difficulty in attaining my goals. Starting today, may I confidently embrace my divine achievements, in the name of Jesus, AMEN.

Personal Prayers Journal

....

....

....

....

....

....

....

Day 237

*"For they all saw him, and were troubled. And immediately he talked with them, and saith unto them, **Be of good cheer: it is I; be not afraid**" (Mark 6:50).*

There is an assurance of safety when the Lord is with me, so I need not fear any fiery darts of Satan coming my way.

———————————

May the presence of God be with me always. May every spirit of fear be cast out from their secret places and replaced with the abiding faith of His presence today, in Jesus' name, AMEN.

Personal Prayers Journal

....

....

....

....

....

....

....

....

....

Day 238

"But the LORD said to Samuel, Do not look at his appearance or at the height of his stature, because I have rejected him"
(1 Samuel 16:7).

I am conscious of what I allow to dwell in my heart because only the Lord knows and sees the content of my heart.

_____

May the content of my heart not disqualify me on the day of my lifting. May the Lord find me faithful always. May only pleasant and pleasing thoughts that glorify the Father fill my mind daily. May I never be rejected but be approved for blessings wherever my name is mentioned from today, in Jesus' Name, AMEN.

Personal Prayers Journal

....

....

....

....

....

....

....

Day 239

"Open my eyes so that I may behold Wonderful things from Your law" (Psalms 119:18).

A blind eye is not only limited to those with physical visual impairment, but it can also refer to someone with a closed mind.

May my understanding be enlightened every day. May my eyes never lose their brightness and always function through divine inspiration. May I see and experience the tangible proof of the grace and glory of His presence on a daily basis. In Jesus' Name, AMEN.

Personal Prayers Journal

....

....

....

....

....

....

....

....

Day 240

*"**Enlarge the place of thy tent**, and let them stretch forth the curtains of thine habitations: spare not, lengthen thy cords, and strengthen thy stakes" (Isaiah 54:2).*

God's commandment to me is never burdensome; obedience to His word brings forth blessings and breakthroughs.

_____

As I take a leap of faith today, may doors of victory and elevation open for me effortlessly. May my territory expand in all directions – to the West, to the East, to the North, and to the South. I will be pursued and never be considered obsolete, discarded, or stagnant from this day forward, in Jesus' Name, AMEN.

Personal Prayers Journal

....

....

....

....

....

....

....

Day 241

"I cannot go in these, he said to Saul, because I am not used to them. So he took them off" (1Samuel 17:39).

David was spiritually connected and sensitive, knowing that he could not overcome any obstacle or defeat a giant with armor made by man.

———————————

May my spirit and mind be alert to receive divine directions and to avoid wrong counsel that leads to destruction. May the Lord divinely help and guide me to overcome any giant in my path. May my spiritual antenna not lose the spiritual signal and connection to receive the word of life from the Father today. May I never be a casualty of any set up of man to waste my life today, in Jesus Name, AMEN.

Personal Prayers Journal

....

....

....

....

....

....

Day 242

"For the LORD sees not as man sees; for man looks at the outward appearance, but the LORD looks at the heart"
(1 Samuel 16:7).

The Lord is the creator of all beings and possesses complete knowledge about each and every aspect of His Creation.

––––––––––––––––

May the Lord always find my heart's contents pleasing. May His loving gaze discover and bless me eternally. May the contents of my heart attract God's favor towards me today. May my thoughts and outward appearance lead me to a place of prosperity, in Jesus' Name, AMEN.

Personal Prayers Journal

....

....

....

....

....

....

....

....

Day 243

"and so after He had patiently endured, He obtained the promise" (Hebrews 6:15).

Patience is a virtue that brings great rewards. Those who practice patience never end up disappointed.

Today, I pray for the grace and tenacity to wait patiently. May I receive all the promises and blessings from the Father. May I not rush and miss out on my share of blessings today, in Jesus' name, AMEN.

Personal Prayers Journal

....

....

....

....

....

....

....

....

....

Day 244

*"Enlarge the place of thy tent, and let them **stretch forth the curtains of thine habitations: spare not**, lengthen thy cords, and strengthen thy stakes" (Isaiah 54:2).*

Divine instruction completed with obedience is a step towards receiving from God. Partial obedience is considered disobedience.'

May the grace to align my day with God's plan and purpose be released to me today. As I stretch out in faith, may I receive angelic help to open the door to success and breakthrough today, in Jesus' Name, AMEN.

Personal Prayers Journal

....

....

....

....

....

....

....

....

Day 245

*"Enlarge the place of thy tent, and let them stretch forth the curtains of thine habitations: spare not, **lengthen thy cords, and strengthen thy stakes**" (Isaiah 54:2).*

The purpose of stretching out my faith is to rely on God's unwavering faith in order to accomplish everything He sets before me.

May all of my steps be purposeful, with the spirit of accomplishment and success guiding me. May I experience multiple harvests as I reset, restart, readjust, refocus, and resume my pursuit of an intimate relationship and reconnection with the Lord today, in Jesus' Name, AMEN.

Personal Prayers Journal

....

....

....

....

....

....

....

Day 246

"Therefore the Lord himself shall give you a sign; Behold, a virgin shall conceive, and bear a son, and shall call his name Immanuel" (Isaiah 7:14).

A sign from God is evidence of His presence and His direction always leads to a testimony of success because He back up His word to perform it.

May I receive spiritual insight and guidance that leads to success today. As I seek counsel from God, may I leave His presence feeling satisfied, fulfilled, and victorious, in Jesus' Name, AMEN.

Personal Prayers Journal

....

....

....

....

....

....

....

....

Day 247

"For thou shalt break forth on the right hand and on the left; and thy seed shall inherit the Gentiles, and make the desolate cities to be inhabited" (Isaiah 54:3).

All-round expansion and enlargement are promised to all of God's children who abides in Him.

May the word of God be fulfilled and accomplished accurately in a my life today. May I increase, multiply, stretch out, and conquer territories for God today, in Jesus' Name, AMEN.

Personal Prayers Journal

....

....

....

....

....

....

....

....

....

Day 248

*"For thou shalt break forth on the right hand and on the left; **And your descendants will take possession of nations And will inhabit deserted cities**" (Isaiah 54:3).*

The covenant blessings of God's children extend to a thousand generations, and He promises these blessings to all our descendants as we guide them to always serve and walk with God.

———————————

May the legacy of His goodness and mercy be passed down to my children's children. May men arise to uplift my descendants to great heights. Let divine helpers enter through unexpected doors and let nations seek counsel from my lineage, starting today, in Jesus' name, AMEN.

Personal Prayers Journal

....

....

....

....

....

....

Day 249

"Therefore I say to you, whatsoever you ask when you pray, believe that you receive them, and you will have them" (Mark12:24).

Faith as small as a mustard seed can move mountains, so I need to protect my heart from any spirit of fear and nurture my faith.

———————————

May I receive the kind of faith that brings instant answers to prayers. As I am still asking, may the window of heaven open over me and shower me with blessings. May my faith and beliefs attract angelic visitation for me today, in Jesus' Name, AMEN.

Personal Prayers Journal

....

....

....

....

....

....

....

Day 250

"Therefore I say to you, whatsoever you ask when you pray,
believe that you receive them, and you will have them"
(Mark12:24).

My faith assures me that nothing is impossible with God, and my belief opens the door to manifest my miracles.

————————————————

May I receive all the answers to every question, thought, or imagination today. May the Lord unlock all delayed opportunities for me today. May my season of waiting come to an end today as I enter the next level of happiness, blessings, and favor, starting from today, in Jesus' Name, AMEN.

Personal Prayers Journal

....

....

....

....

....

....

....

....

Day 251

"Keep your heart with all diligence, for out of it springs the issues of life" (Proverbs 4:23).

The eyes and ears serve as the gateways to the mind, soul, and spirit. Therefore, what I allow into them is a reflection of my thoughts and speech on a daily basis.

———————————

May my heart be filled solely with uplifting thoughts. May I never listen to the words of strangers that could steer me away from my purpose. As I speak, may my heart be filled with the words of life that nourish and uplift all who hear them. May my eyes only perceive the goodness of God today and always. In Jesus' name, AMEN.

Personal Prayers Journal

....

....

....

....

....

....

....

Day 252

"You who hear and answer prayer, To You all people will come"
(Psalms 65:2).

It is crucial to know who to turn to in times of distress or desperation. There should never be another option when we are fully devoted to Jesus Christ.

As I stand in the presence of the King of kings and Lord of lords today, may my heartfelt plea captures the attention of the heavenly hosts. May my prayers be answered without delay or denial, and may any spiritual obstacles hindering the fulfillment of my requests be removed. May my joy overflow with endless testimonies of answered prayers today, in Jesus' Name, AMEN.

Personal Prayers Journal

....

....

....

....

....

....

Day 253

"But you, be strong and do not let your hands be weak: for your work shall be rewarded" (2 Chronicles 15:7).

A diligent and determined mind accomplishes more than one can imagine with the Lord's support.

———————————————

May I be granted the grace to persist and persevere today. May my hands always be strengthened. May I be fruitful in every good work and never labor in vain again, as my heart is shaped and dedicated to God's kingdom agenda. May I receive abundant rewards from God, who answers prayers, today. In Jesus' Name, AMEN.

Personal Prayers Journal

....

....

....

....

....

....

....

....

Day 254

*"**He fashioneth their hearts alike**; he considereth all their works" (Psalms 33:15).*

God intentionally and decisively uses His creative abilities to craft us uniquely for His pleasure.

———————

May my life daily reflect His glory. May my uniqueness and grateful heart draw people closer to God. The transformation that comes with His presence in me will be visible to everyone. As I focus on pleasing Him daily, the Lord will make me a wonder to my generation. In Jesus' Name, AMEN.

Personal Prayers Journal

....

....

....

....

....

....

....

....

Day 255

*"He fashioneth their hearts alike; **he considereth all their works**" (Psalms 33:15).*

The God we serve is a rewarder of all those who seek Him, and serving God is always remembered and rewarded.

May the Lord remember all my labor of love in His vineyard from this day forward. May my sacrifices open great doors for me. May my works not be in vain during times of testing and endurance. May I receive double blessings for my troubles today, in Jesus' Name, AMEN.

Personal Prayers Journal

....

....

....

....

....

....

....

....

....

Day 256

"Did I not choose him out of all the tribes of Israel to be my priest" (1 Samuel 2:28).

The selection for kingdom work is not based on position, rank, or man's approval, but rather on the guidance of the Holy Spirit.

I pray that the Lord considers me worthy of His divine appointment. May I be chosen and singled out from the crowd for divine promotion and elevation. May my role as a priest never lack anointing. May my priestly garments remain intact, untarnished, and undefiled. May they never be taken away, exchanged, or occupied by another person from this day forward, in the name of Jesus. Amen.

Personal Prayers Journal

....

....

....

....

....

....

Day 257

"When he hesitated, the angel grasped his hands, his wife's and daughter's hands, and led them safety out of the city"
(Genesis 19:16).

The Lord's unmerited favor, divine selection, and His mercies protect and prevent calamity and destruction.

May the hand of the Lord daily guide and guard my ways. May I hear only God's voice leading me through the path of life. Let God be merciful and gracious, pulling me out of any danger and rescuing me from calamity today, in Jesus' Name, AMEN.

Personal Prayers Journal

....

....

....

....

....

....

....

....

Day 258

"Do not be deceived; evil company corrupts good manners" (1 Corinthians 15:33).

Having a relationship with the Lord guarantees having the best companion one could ever have. On the other hand, partnering with the devil ultimately leads to eternal damnation and destruction.

I pray to be able to dwell in God's presence and be recognized as one of God's beloved. May I never be found among sinners or in the company of those who are scornful. I ask the Lord to separate me from anyone who will not bring value to my life. May I never associate myself with individuals who hinder progress, cause stagnation, or seek to disrupt my destiny, in Jesus' Name, AMEN.

Personal Prayers Journal

....

....

....

....

....

....

Day 259

"No one having put their hands on the ploy, and looking back, is fit for God's kingdom" (Luke 9:62).

Discipline, determination, and diligence are keys to walking with God and worshiping Him through our daily service and it is important to avoid doubt and distraction.

May the Lord grant me the grace and tenacity to serve Him. May I be shielded from challenges or distractions that can hinder my progress and prevent me from reaping the rewards of my service. May my worship be recognized as fitting and appropriate, leading to both physical and eternal rewards from our Father, who gives good gifts to all His children. In Jesus' name, AMEN.

Personal Prayers Journal

....

....

....

....

....

....

Day 260

"And we know that all things work together for good to them that love God, to them who are the called according to his purpose" (Romans 8:28).

The understanding of God's identity brings about tranquility and a sense of total well-being for all those dear to Him.

May all of God's prophecies, declarations, promises, plans, and purposes for me be perfectly fulfilled today. May every aspect of my life align for my benefit each day. May any unfavorable intentions be turned in my favor as I consistently experience the Lord's goodness today and forevermore, in Jesus' name, AMEN.

Personal Prayers Journal

....

....

....

....

....

....

....

....

Day 261

*"And we know that all things work together for good to them that love God, **to them who are the called according to his purpose**" (Romans 8:28).*

The calling of God on anyone is a setup for elevation and greatness. Listen for and respond to the call.

———————————————

May the purpose of my calling and chosen path as a child of God be fulfilled. Let my divine assignment be accomplished effortlessly; may I never encounter frustration in fulfilling my calling. May my destiny helpers align my path for divine assistance towards achieving greatness today, in Jesus' name, AMEN.

Personal Prayers Journal

....

....

....

....

....

....

....

Day 262

*"**But the wisdom that is from above is first pure, then peaceable**; but the wisdom that is from above is gentle, willing to yield, full of mercy and good fruits, but the wisdom that is from above is without partiality and without hypocrisy"*
(James 3:17).

Our God is full of wisdom and knowledge. He is willing to give wisdom to anyone who desires it.

_____May I always be filled with the spirit of wisdom and may I avoid the counsel of fools. May my life be a mystery that cannot be unraveled by men. May I experience the refreshing knowledge and wisdom in His presence today and always, in Jesus' Name, AMEN.

Personal Prayers Journal

....

....

....

....

....

....

....

Day 263

*"But the wisdom that is from above is first pure, then peaceable; **but the wisdom that is from above is gentle, willing to yield, full of mercy and good fruits,** but the wisdom that is from above is without partiality and without hypocrisy" (James 3:17).*

The Spirit of God is quiet and gentle, providing correction and counsel. The Spirit resides in the still small voice, not in noise.

———————————

May the Lord anoint me with fresh oil today. As I go about my day, may I experience only the mercy, grace, and goodness of God. May I bear good fruits and have a bountiful harvest in various aspects of my life today, in Jesus' Name. Amen.

Personal Prayers Journal

....

....

....

....

....

....

Day 264

*"But the wisdom that is from above is first pure, then peaceable; but the wisdom that is from above is gentle, willing to yield, full of mercy and good fruits, **but the wisdom that is from above is without partiality and without hypocrisy** (James 3:17).*

Our God does not show favoritism and is faithful to everyone who comes to Him. He generously gives to those who ask Him.

May my voice be heard for immediate blessings today. May I receive divine help and answers to my prayers every day. Lord, please guide me with divine wisdom that surpasses human understanding, starting today. In Jesus' Name, Amen.

Personal Prayers Journal

....

....

....

....

....

....

Day 265

*"**But thou, when thou prayest, enter into thy closet**, and when thou hast shut thy door, pray to thy Father which is in secret; and thy Father which seeth in secret shall reward thee openly" (Matthew 6:6).*

Vulgarity has no association with our God, as He sees and responds to all of our prayers, including the desires of our hearts.

———————————

May my requests to the Almighty Father be given urgent attention today. May the Lord answer me while I am still speaking. May my tears be wiped away and replaced with songs of joy and thanksgiving. Let me receive answers to long-awaited prayer requests today, in Jesus' Name, AMEN.

Personal Prayers Journal

....

....

....

....

....

....

....

Day 266

*"But thou, when thou prayest, enter into thy closet, and when thou hast shut thy door, **pray to thy Father which is in secret; and thy Father which seeth in secret shall reward thee openly**" (Matthew 6:6).*

God is the one who reveals secrets and understands the deepest parts of our being - our hearts, bodies, minds, and souls. In His presence, everything about us is laid bare, like an open book.

I pray that the Lord will grant me access to the treasures of darkness and the hidden riches of secret places. May I receive the rewards for all the acts of love I have done in His service, starting from today. I pray this in the name of Jesus, AMEN.

Personal Prayers Journal

....

....

....

....

....

....

Day 267

"And I will delight myself in Your commandments, which I love" (Psalms 119:47).

The Lord is pleased and rejoices when we take delight in Him, just as a good child brings joy to the heart of their father.

May the Lord find joy in my obedience and love for Him. May my songs of praise and worship rise up like a sweet fragrance, unlocking doors of kindness for me. May my actions and behavior bring daily joy in the presence of the Lord from this day onwards, in Jesus' Name, AMEN.

Personal Prayers Journal

....

....

....

....

....

....

....

....

Day 268

"My hands also I will lift up to Your commandments,
which I love, and I will meditate on Your statutes"
(Psalms 119:48).

Lifting our hands in worship is an act of complete surrender and dependence on the Lord.

May the Lord reciprocate my total dependence on Him with showers of blessings. Let me receive pleasant surprises in the midst of my worship and adoration of the Father today, in Jesus' Name, Amen.

Personal Prayers Journal

....

....

....

....

....

....

....

....

Day 269

*"My hands also I will lift up to Your commandments, which I love, **and I will meditate on Your statutes**"*
(Psalms 119:48).

God's commandment for His beloved is to bring blessings, not harm or hurt. Meditating on and living by His word will guarantee a secure blessing from Him.

May the Word of God become alive and testify in my life today. May the reality and actualization of His word guide and lead me to a place of favor. May the Rhema of His word, which is fast, powerful, and sharper than a two-edged sword, pave the way for my breakthroughs today, in Jesus' Name, AMEN.

Personal Prayers Journal

....

....

....

....

....

....

Day 270

*"**And when Jesus was passed over again by ship unto the other side**, much people gathered unto him: and he was nigh unto the sea" (Mark 5:21).*

A purposeful step must be taken to cross over obstacles because there is beauty in exchange for ashes and joy in exchange for mourning on the other side.

———————————————

May I successfully navigate every crossroad of hindrance, limitation, and stagnation today. May any obstacles in my path be removed as I break through and enter into a new period of triumph. May my steps be guided and aligned with God's plan for me today, in Jesus' Name, AMEN.

Personal Prayers Journal

....

....

....

....

....

....

....

Day 271

*"And when Jesus was passed over again by ship unto the other side, **much people gathered unto him: and he was nigh unto the sea**" (Mark 5:21).*

I must stay connected to the source of life in order to live, just like many people gather to Jesus because He is the source of life.

As I consistently align myself with God's plans each day, may others come together to rejoice in my blessings. May I experience the power of God and receive divine provisions every day, in Jesus' Name, Amen.

Personal Prayers Journal

....

....

....

....

....

....

....

....

Day 272

"For thou hast girded me with strength unto the battle:
thou hast subdued under me those that rose up against me"
(Psalms 18: 39).

Partnership with Jesus will always yield a hundred percent increase and ensure victory. I am always victorious when the Lord partners with me.

May the Lord lead and partner with me in the battles of life. May God defeat all my enemies and destroy anyone who plans my downfall today. Let me not fail or become prey to my adversaries. May I experience complete victory in His everlasting arms as He protects me daily. May His strength be made perfect in any area of weakness today, in Jesus' Name, Amen.

Personal Prayers Journal

....

....

....

....

....

Day 273

*"For thou hast girded me with strength unto the battle: **thou hast subdued under me those that rose up against me** "*
(Psalms 18: 39).

The Lord is jealous over all His beloved and defends, protects, and silence every voice of opposition against me.

––––––––––––––––––––––

May I be counted as one of His beloved today. Let the Lord be jealous over me. May all my enemies be subdued by the armies of the living God. May the enemies that rise against me flee in seven different ways. May dangers, doubts, destructions, and death be subdued before me today, in Jesus' Name, AMEN.

Personal Prayers Journal

....

....

....

....

....

....

....

Day 274

*"**Thou art my King, O God**: command deliverances for Jacob"* (Psalms 44:4).

My recognition and acknowledgement of the Lordship of Jesus renders all other kings powerless in my life.

May every king that causes trouble for me be dethroned. Lord, rescue and save me from every king that frustrates the grace and glory of God on my life. May every tongue of condemnation and contempt be silenced over me today, in Jesus' Name, AMEN.

Personal Prayers Journal

....

....

....

....

....

....

....

....

Day 275

*"Thou art my King, O God: **command deliverances for Jacob**" (Psalms 44:4).*

I have the authority, as a seed of Abraham, Isaac, and Jacob, to ask anything of the Lord, and I am confident that He will respond quickly.

I pray that heaven will release and deliver all of my blessings to me today. I ask that any delays or feelings of despair in my life be transformed by divine intervention, leading to a breakthrough today. May the Lord find me and make me a living testimony of miracles, signs, and wonders today. I declare that I will receive great deliverance for myself and my household, and I will rejoice with shouts of joy today, in Jesus' Name, AMEN.

Personal Prayers Journal

....

....

....

....

....

....

Day 276

*"**He brought me forth also into a large place**; he delivered me, because he delighted in me" (Psalms 18:19).*

When God carries you, you are able to see and experience things that others cannot. It allows your vision to expand beyond what your physical capacity can perceive.

I pray that the Lord guides and directs me to the place where my blessings abound. I no longer want to be seen as insignificant, small, or limited. I ask that any state of stagnation be reversed as I continue to grow and expand in all areas of my life, starting from today. In Jesus' Name, AMEN.

Personal Prayers Journal

....

....

....

....

....

....

....

Day 277

"It is God that girdeth me with strength, and makes my way perfect" (Psalms 18:32).

We are assured of God's strength in all areas of weakness, as this promise is given to all His children.

May the Lord be my strength and shield each day. May His presence be a constant protection, guarding me from the front and rear. May His powerful hands remove any obstacles that stand in the way of my success. Lord, guide me on the right path, away from failure, distress, oppression, sorrow, calamity, sickness, and hardship as I go about my day. In Jesus' Name, AMEN.

Personal Prayers Journal

....

....

....

....

....

....

....

Day 278

"The Lord rewarded me according to my righteousness; according to the cleanness of my hands hath he recompensed me" (Psalms 18:20).

The Lord remembers and rewards every diligent and faithful service in His vineyard. Do not grow weary of doing good.

May the Lord bless my service abundantly. May I receive the grace to use my talents and resources to serve Him even more today. May I experience an increase in congratulations and favor from today onwards, in Jesus' Name, AMEN.

Personal Prayers Journal

....

....

....

....

....

....

....

....

Day 279

*"The Lord rewarded me according to my righteousness; **according to the cleanness of my hands hath he recompensed me**" (Psalms 18:20).*

God prospers and rewards the integrity, hard work, obedience, diligence, honesty, and commitment of all His children.

May His mighty hands distinguish me from my contemporaries. May today be the day I emergeinto the limelight. May I not labor in vain, and may little effort produce abundance by Your favor today, in Jesus' Name, AMEN.

Personal Prayers Journal

....

....

....

....

....

....

....

....

Day 280

"Thou hast delivered me from the strivings of the people"
(Psalms 18:43).

We serve a God who is mightier than any man of war. He saves, protects, and delivers us from the arrows and darts of the enemy.

———————————————

May the great deliverer visit my current situation and every unpleasant circumstance in my life today. Let today be the end of all unpleasantness, contention, and strife caused by others against me. Let Jehovah El-Gibbor and Jehovah Sabbaoth fight for me until all my enemies are destroyed. May every attack against me become a stepping-stone to my success today, in Jesus' Name, AMEN.

Personal Prayers Journal

....

....

....

....

....

....

Day 281

"It is God that avengeth me, and subdueth the people under me" (Psalms 18:47).

One of the most reassuring facts about God is that He fights most of our battles without our knowledge.

———————————————

May God arise to defend me. May every gathering against my progress today be scattered. Let God descend on my enemies as they gather to attack me today. May any hand pointed in my direction for evil wither; they shall not be able to perform their enterprise against me. May enemies of progress be subdued under me today, in Jesus' Name, AMEN.

Personal Prayers Journal

....

....

....

....

....

....

....

Day 282

"Thou hast enlarged my steps under me, that my feet did not slip" (Psalms 18:36).

Stability comes from God, as He aligns the steps of His righteous ones to enlarge and prosper their ways.

May my feet lead me to the palace and never to the pit. May my feet be firmly planted and established on the unshakable rock. Let my steps align with divine purpose to bring forth the breakthrough I desire today, in Jesus' name. Amen.

Personal Prayers Journal

....

....

....

....

....

....

....

....

....

Day 283

"The Lord liveth; and blessed be my rock; and let the God of my salvation be exalted" (Psalms 18:46).

The keys to accessing the throne room of God's presence are found in the fruits of our lips: adoration, praise, and worship with thanksgiving to my God and Lord.

Today, may I receive the key to enter the Holy of Holies and worship in Spirit and in Truth. I pray that the heavens over my head remain permanently open. May the God of my salvation be exalted in every situation today, in Jesus' Name, AMEN.

Personal Prayers Journal

....

....

....

....

....

....

....

....

Day 284

*"As soon as they hear of me, they shall obey me: **the strangers shall submit themselves unto me**" (Psalms 18:44).*

The light of God's presence within me cannot be concealed; it illuminates and guides me to fulfill my purpose in this generation.

May men be raised up to support and elevate me to positions of influence and importance. May all forces of darkness be expelled from their hidden strongholds when they encounter me. Similar to Joseph, may all those who seek to harm and undermine me be humbled in my presence. From this day forward, even strangers will willingly submit themselves to me, in the name of Jesus, AMEN.

Personal Prayers Journal

....

....

....

....

....

....

Day 285

*"**As soon as they hear of me, they shall obey me**: the strangers shall submit themselves unto me" (Psalms 18:44).*

My voice carries power and authority because of the name of Jesus and the Holy Spirit working inside me.

May men eagerly seek my aid and attention. May my presence attract favor and blessings to me on a daily basis. May my introduction to my generation prompt men to recognize my relevance and position me accordingly. In Jesus' name, amen.

Personal Prayers Journal

....

....

....

....

....

....

....

....

....

Day 286

"Thou hast delivered me from the strivings of the people; and thou hast made me the head of the heathen: a people whom I have not known shall serve me" (Psalms 18:43).

God is my savior because He saved and delivered me from destruction. Hence, when I am on God's side, complete victory is assured.

May the Lord justify me and put my accusers to shame. I shall daily report victory over every evil agenda of the devil, attempting to halt my achievements. Let the Lord set an ambush against my enemies and cause them to turn against themselves, leading to my complete victory today, in Jesus' Name, AMEN.

Personal Prayers Journal

....

....

....

....

....

....

Day 287

*"Thou hast delivered me from the strivings of the people; **and thou hast made me the head of the heathen**: a people whom I have not known shall serve me"* (Psalms 18:43).

The Lord is the one who enthrones, empowers, and establishes individuals in positions of leadership, even in the face of plotting and agitation from others.

I humbly ask to receive the mantle and grace to reign and rule over nations today. Please release the key that will unlock the doors to my place of elevation. May nations come together to rejoice in my achievements. May kings arise and proclaim me as the blessed and favored one of God, starting today in Jesus' name, AMEN.

Personal Prayers Journal

....

....

....

....

....

....

Day 288

"He delivered me, because he delighted in me"
(Psalms 18:19)

God not only delights in delivering us from our enemies, but also in bringing shame and confusion to those who rise up against us.

May the Lord grant all of my desires as I find delight in Him today. May my heart, mind, and soul be pleasing to the Father today and always. In Jesus' name, may God command great deliverance for me and everything that belongs to me in all areas. AMEN.

Personal Prayers Journal

....

....

....

....

....

....

....

Day 289

*"Thou hast delivered me from the strivings of the people; and thou hast made me the head of the heathen: **a people whom I have not known shall serve me**" (Psalms 18:43).*

The God we serve has the ability to uplift and place me in a position of honor and dignity, even among foreigners, in order to bring glory to His name.

May my service serve as a means to unlock the door and capture the attention of heavenly hosts and mortal men, in order to receive favor. May the doors of favor and divine blessings never be closed to me. As I dedicate myself to serving God, He will raise others to serve me. I accept the key to accessing numerous doors of reward for my service, in Jesus' Name. AMEN.

Personal Prayers Journal

....

....

....

....

....

....

Day 290

"She anointed the feet of Jesus, and wiped His feet with her hair. And the house was filled with the fragrance of the oil"
(John 12:3).

Our sacrifice, adoration, and genuine worship attract the attention and Shekinah glory of the Father.

Today, may I encounter divine visitation in the place of worship. May my tears of sorrow be transformed into tears of joy. May the fragrance of favor and the oil of gladness bring healing to my heart, soul, and mind, in the name of Jesus. AMEN.

Personal Prayers Journal

....

....

....

....

....

....

....

....

Day 291

"The Lord bless, keep and shine His glory on you"
(Numbers 6:24).

No one can undo the blessings and divine declarations that God has spoken over his children.

Today, I confidently declare and decree that I am blessed. May the promises of God concerning me be fulfilled with precision today. May my light continue to shine brightly and may God's glory in my life never be hidden. I pray that today, I will receive the Lord's blessings that elevate me from a place of normalcy to a position of extraordinary success. In Jesus' name, AMEN.

Personal Prayers Journal

....

....

....

....

....

....

....

Day 292

"You open Your hand and satisfy the desire of every living thing" (Psalms 145;16).

An open hand is capable of both giving and receiving, while a closed fist cannot do either.

May I always be embraced by the loving and powerful arms of the Lord. May He carry me so that I do not fall or stumble. Let Him lift me above the storms of life to a place of joy and peace. May God fulfill my desires with all good things. My hands are open to bless others and to receive blessings from the Lord, who is the giver of good gifts. In Jesus' name, AMEN.

Personal Prayers Journal

....

....

....

....

....

....

....

Day 293

"Saul looked at David with suspicion and jealously from that day forward" (1 Samuel 18:9).

The Lord continues to uplift the hands of the righteous, even in the face of the wicked's evil intentions.

———————————

May all those who gather against me be scattered. I am impervious to any attacks from those who rise against me. May every evil plan to confuse, manipulate, or steal my joy pass over me. May God's shield and protective covering rest upon me. Let every wicked eye that gazes upon me be struck with permanent blindness. May the schemes of those who seek to bring frustration and shame into my life be reversed today, in Jesus' name. AMEN.

Personal Prayers Journal

....

....

....

....

....

....

....

Day 294

"Now Saul was afraid of David, because the LORD was with him, but had departed from Saul" (1 Samuel 18:12).

God partners with all His obedient children. When we choose a life of sin and disobedience, we walk out of His presence.

May the Lord's presence always cover and protect me, serving as a front and rear guard. May He always lead, guide, and protect me. May my enemies tremble in dread and fear, as they see me standing firm. May their plans to harm me be frustrated, returning upon their own heads. May God arise on my behalf, bringing shame and confusion to all my enemies today, in Jesus' Name, AMEN.

Personal Prayers Journal

....

....

....

....

....

....

....

Day 295

"Now it was on a Sabbath day that Jesus made the mud and opened the man's eyes" (John 9:14).

God is always punctual and not bound by dates, times, or seasons. Time begins with God and ends with the ticking of man's clock.

May the Lord visit and meet all of my needs today. No human laws or restrictions will hinder my breakthrough or testimony. Let heaven and earth join together with the Father's voice to release everything that is owed to me today. May my spiritual eyes be opened and remain open. Let any lifelong shame and stigma from the past be reversed, in Jesus' Name, AMEN.

Personal Prayers Journal

....

....

....

....

....

....

Day 296

*"**God is not a man, that he should lie** neither is He the son of man, that he should repent. Hath he said it, and shall he not do it? Has he spoken, and shall he not make it good?"*
(Numbers 23:19)

Our God is described as the Way, the Truth, and the Life. Therefore, whatever He says remains permanent; nothing can be added or removed.

May the word of God overthrow every lie that man has spoken about me. May the Lord bring accurate fulfillment to all His promises concerning me. May my life serve as a reference point and a testimony today, in Jesus' name. Amen.

Personal Prayers Journal

....

....

....

....

....

....

....

Day 297

*"God is not a man, that he should lie **neither is He the son of man, that he should repent.** Hath he said it, and shall he not do it? Has he spoken, and shall he not make it good?"*
(Numbers 23:19)

God is truly and completely honest, so whatever He says about me will surely happen.

May the Lord forgive any sins from my past that could hinder my blessings. May my past mistakes not delay or prevent my breakthrough today. May the covenant in the blood of Jesus remove any accusations against the blessings meant for me, in Jesus' Name, AMEN.

Personal Prayers Journal

....

....

....

....

....

....

....

Day 298

*"God is not a man, that he should lie neither is He the son of man, that he should repent. **Hath he said it, and shall he not do it?** Has he spoken, and shall he not make it good?"*
(Numbers 23:19)

God does not use empty words like humans do. Whatever He says will be fulfilled at the right time.

May the Lord grant me a testimony that will leave everyone amazed today. May I receive unexpected good news that will bring solutions to my long-standing problems. May I be overwhelmed by blessings as the Lord multiplies all the blessings He has planned for me today, in Jesus' name, AMEN.

Personal Prayers Journal

....

....

....

....

....

Day 299

*"God is not a man, that he should lie neither is He the son of man, that he should repent. Hath he said it, and shall he not do it? **Has he spoken, and shall he not make it good?**"*
(Numbers 23:19)

The word of God is never in vain. It is like a seed planted in fertile soil that God nurtures and cares for until it bears fruit.

May every word of life spoken over me be watered and sprout to bring blessings and breakthroughs for me. Let the promises spoken over me never remain dormant. May the power of God's word break through all obstacles and barriers today. May God's word come to fruition, and may I experience daily testimonies of joy, in Jesus' name, AMEN.

Personal Prayers Journal

....

....

....

....

....

....

....

Day 300

"I will extol and praise You, O LORD, for You have lifted me up, you have not let my enemies rejoice over me" *(Psalms 30:1).*

God dwells in the praise of His children, so I will praise and exalt Him to invite His presence.

May the glorious presence of God cover me as I raise my voice in praise and adoration today. Let the eternal and mighty arms of the Lord carry me through life's storms. May the all-powerful God lift me above fear, shame, and pain. Let my mouth and heart be filled with joy and gladness from this day forward, in Jesus' Name, AMEN.

Personal Prayers Journal

....

....

....

....

....

....

....

Day 301

*"I will extol and praise You, O LORD, for You have lifted me up, **you have not let my enemies rejoice over me**"*
(Psalms 30:1).

The presence of God in a believer's life guarantees a life filled with unending joy, indescribable joy, and joy that overflows to others.

May the Lord display His presence in my life just as He faithfully shows up for me. May my situation never be forgotten, delayed, or dismissed. May my enemies not gather to question the whereabouts of my God or find satisfaction in my circumstances. May the Lord unsettle and humiliate all those who come against me today and always, in Jesus' name, AMEN.

Personal Prayers Journal

....

....

....

....

....

....

Day 302

*"**Thy kingdom come**. Thy will be done in earth, as it is in heaven". (Matthew 6:10).*

God's Kingdom is established forever on earth just as it is in heaven. No other kingdom has the authority to operate or be established.

Today, may the kingdom of God be established in every situation of my life. Let the kingdom of men that causes unpleasant situations in my life be dethroned once and for all. May the Shekinah glory of Christ cover me every day and elevate me above any man-made throne and kingdoms occupied by principalities and powers. In Jesus' Name, AMEN.

Personal Prayers Journal

....

....

....

....

....

....

Day 303

*"Thy kingdom come. **Thy will be done in earth, as it is in heaven**" (Matthew 6:10).*

The kingdom of God encompasses both heaven and earth, and His will and voice supersede any human will.

May only God's perfect will, rather than what is merely permissible, manifest in my life. May all selfish desires and actions driven by human nature be eliminated. May I experience God's will to prosper and be in good health today. May I be empowered to lend to nations and not borrow. May I receive God's heavenly mandate to be above all, as I rule and reign with Christ starting today, in the name of Jesus, AMEN.

Personal Prayers Journal

....

....

....

....

....

....

Day 304

"But when he saw Jesus afar off, he ran and worshipped him"
(Mark 5: 6).

The glory and radiance of God are impossible to overlook or disregard. They create a strong desire in people to bow down and worship Him.

I pray that the glory of God in my life will not go unnoticed. May His presence within me attract individuals who will aid me in fulfilling my destiny. May my life become a magnet for favor. May all negative influences from the past surrender and contribute to my progress. May I be chosen for blessings, and may influential people come forward to assist me in reaching my rightful position today, in Jesus' Name, Amen.

Personal Prayers Journal

....

....

....

....

....

Day 305

"And he said unto her, Daughter, thy faith hath made thee whole; go in peace, and be whole of thy plague" (Mark 5:34).

Faith is the belief and connection to the realization of the unimaginable and the trust that God is the healer and guarantor of complete wholeness.

As I connect with Him in faith today, may every affliction tormenting my life come to an end. I receive my divine encounter of healing and restoration today. Let every death sentence over me be reversed and replaced with an increase in the length of my days and years on earth, in Jesus' Name, AMEN.

Personal Prayers Journal

....

....

....

....

....

....

Day 306

*"And he said unto her, Daughter, thy faith hath made thee whole; **go in peace, and be whole of thy plague**"*
(Mark 5:34).

The declaration and assurance of peace comes when it is spoken by the Prince of Peace Himself, and it cannot be reversed.

May the Lord silence and calm every storm of sickness and affliction in my life. Let the Great Physician remove every pain and distress and make me whole, as every negative voice of infirmity is silenced. May every day of my life be peaceful as I partner with the Prince of Peace today, in Jesus' Name. AMEN.

Personal Prayers Journal

....

....

....

....

....

....

Day 307

*"**And all the earth sought to Solomon**, to hear his wisdom, which God had put in his heart" (1 Kings 10:24)*

You must possess something that attracts others to your presence and motivates them to seek your counsel and guidance.

_____

May my radiance lead people to Christ. May Kings and Queens be captivated by the glorious light of His presence within me. I will not be rejected, but rather sought after from this day forward, in Jesus' name, AMEN.

Personal Prayers Journal

....

....

....

....

....

....

....

....

Day 308

"And all the earth sought to Solomon, to hear his wisdom, which God had put in his heart" (1 Kings 10:24)

A man who is filled with godly wisdom holds the power to captivate an audience and command authority, as the wisdom of God surpasses and overrules every human voice.

May men come to me seeking counsel, and may important decisions be made based on my wisdom. May the Lord grant me a message that cannot be disputed by anyone. Let men eagerly gather to listen to my words. May the wisdom that I impart bless not only the current generation, but also future generations yet to come. May God render foolish every word spoken in judgment, condemnation, or attempts to belittle me by my adversaries today, in Jesus' Name, AMEN.

Personal Prayers Journal

....

....

....

....

....

....

Day 309

"And all the earth sought to Solomon, to hear his wisdom, which God had put in his heart" (1 Kings 10:24)

Godly wisdom is the result and reward of being in divine association with the only one who gives wisdom to all those who desire and ask for it.

———————————

May the hand of God rest mightily upon me as I speak with wisdom today. May God fill my heart with His wisdom that attracts others, so that I can be a blessing to all. May the wisdom of God within me cause a supernatural shift for my blessings today. May my life be filled with the grace to speak godly counsel and not foolish words. May I only speak the will and the heart of the Father from this day forth, and may it impact the lives of all who hear, in Jesus' Name, AMEN.

Personal Prayers Journal

....

....

....

....

....

....

Day 310

"The LORD bless and keep you" (Numbers 6:24).

God is the sole and ultimate source of blessings, and no person has the power to alter His words over my life except for myself.

I pray that the Lord blesses the words that come out of my mouth and the thoughts that occupy my heart today. May God provide protection, support, guidance, and safeguard me each day. May the mighty hand of God shield me from any harm or disaster and fulfill all my needs throughout this day. I ask this in Jesus' name, AMEN.

Personal Prayers Journal

....

....

....

....

....

....

....

....

Day 311

"The LORD make His face shine upon you"
(Numbers 6:25).

The presence of God's light eradicates all darkness, surpassing any artificial light created by humans.

May the Lord, be my guiding light, shining through me. May my light attract people and lead them to receive the gift of salvation. May the glorious presence of God favor me, even when I am undeserving. Let anyone who speaks against me and tries to bring me down be judged by God. I am assisted and uplifted to a position of honor, just as Moses stood before Pharaoh, today and always, in Jesus' name, Amen.

Personal Prayers Journal

....

....

....

....

....

....

....

Day 312

"The Lord will be gracious to you" (Numbers 6:25).

Grace is the reason why a man is chosen for undeserved favor. I am a testament to God's grace every time I wake up.

May the Lord envelop me with His loving kindness, so that I no longer have to struggle in life. May the achievements of others become my starting point. May my blessings come to me from unexpected sources. May my daily testimonies reflect the fact that I am uplifted by grace today, in Jesus' Name, AMEN.

Personal Prayers Journal

....

....

....

....

....

....

....

....

....

Day 313

"At Gibeon the LORD appeared to Solomon"
(1 Kings 3:5).

Gibeon is a place of ultimate sacrifice, divine experience, and supernatural encounters.

_____

May the Lord meet me at Gibeon today. May my sacrificial offering draw God's presence towards me. May I not miss the day of my divine visitation. May my encounter at Gibeon be a life-transforming experience today, in Jesus' Name. Amen.

Personal Prayers Journal

....

....

....

....

....

....

....

....

....

Day 314

"The LORD lift His countenance upon you for divine approval" (Numbers 6:26).

I seek God's approval because a person who is approved by God will never be disapproved by other people.

_____

May I never face rejection from others. May the Lord show His approval towards me. May I always be pursued and never be denied, rejected, disqualified, or let down in life. May God's powerful influence on my life prompt others to support me today, in the Name of Jesus, AMEN.

Personal Prayers Journal

....

....

....

....

....

....

....

....

Day 315

"At Gibeon the LORD appeared to Solomon in a dream at night" (1 Kings 3:5).

The manifestation of God's promise begins with a dream and a divine visitation that changes the trajectory of an ordinary life to an extraordinary one.

May the Lord visit me with dreams and revelation knowledge that cause men to bow before the God I serve. May my words not go unheard, but rather be fulfilled accurately and swiftly as soon as they are spoken. May my divine visitation through dreams not fade away, but instead materialize in the physical realm, bringing abundant blessings from the Father today, in Jesus' Name, AMEN.

Personal Prayers Journal

....

....

....

....

....

....

Day 316

*"In Gibeon the LORD appeared to Solomon in a dream by night: **and God said, Ask what I shall give thee**"*
(1 Kings 3:5).

The key to receiving an open request from God, where we can ask for anything, is preceded by a life of complete commitment and self-sacrifice.

From today onward, may I only hear the voice of God. Let every contrary voice be silenced, and may every strange voice that I have heard in the past, which sought to derail my destiny, be permanently silenced over me. From now on, may the voice of God lead and guide me. May God's voice always be louder than any other voice that speaks evil or destruction against me. In Jesus' name, AMEN.

Personal Prayers Journal

....

....

....

....

....

Day 317

"The LORD lift up his countenance upon thee, and give thee peace" (Numbers 6:26).

When a man is in the presence of God and experiences His glory, the man becomes unnoticeable, as God's glory is revealed.

May the Prince of Peace grant me a peaceful remainder of my years. May I experience holistic peace in every aspect of my life - physically, mentally, emotionally, financially, and spiritually. May I be consistently covered by God's abiding glory each day. In Jesus' name, I pray that any rumors or physical signs of war that surround me may be silenced today. Amen.

Personal Prayers Journal

....

....

....

....

....

....

Day 318

*"**And I will bring forth a seed out of Jacob**, and out of Judah an inheritor of my mountains: and mine elect shall inherit it, and my servants shall dwell there"* (Isaiah 65:9).

Seeds are planted with the expectation of bearing fruit, but they require watering, nurturing, and cultivation.

May my seed operate under the Abrahamic covenant of fruitfulness, blessings, and flourishing. Let my seed fall on fertile soil, grow, and germinate into a mighty oak of righteousness. May my seed be watered and bring forth good fruits in all seasons. Let my seed serve the Lord, and may I bear fruit up to a thousand generations from today, in Jesus' Name, AMEN.

Personal Prayers Journal

....

....

....

....

....

....

Day 319

*"In Gibeon the LORD appeared to Solomon in a dream by night: and God said, **Ask what I shall give thee**"*
(1 Kings 3:5).

When the owner of the entire universe wants to bless you, you can be assured of endless success and abundance.

May the Lord be gracious to me as I present my requests to Him today. May I receive answers to all my prayers from the creator of every good and perfect gift. Let my petition to the Father bring forth a lasting covenant of blessings to my life, for generations to come. In Jesus' Name, AMEN.

Personal Prayers Journal

....

....

....

....

....

....

....

....

Day 320

*"**Notwithstanding the Lord stood with me**, and strengthened me; that by me the preaching might be fully known, and that all the Gentiles might hear: and I was delivered out of the mouth of the lion" (2 Timothy 4:17).*

The Lord is our shield and guard. When He stands with us, we are protected from any storm of life.

———————————

May the presence of the Lord chase away every evil force around me. As the Lord stands with me, may mountains be leveled, valleys lifted, and crooked ways straightened. May all powers of darkness flee as I triumph in complete victory today, in Jesus' Name. Amen.

Personal Prayers Journal

....

....

....

....

....

....

....

Day 321

*"And I will bring forth a seed out of Jacob, **and out of Judah an inheritor of my mountains**: and mine elect shall inherit it, and my servants shall dwell there" (Isaiah 65:9).*

The heir is the rightful beneficiary and recipient of everything that belongs to the father, and a heart filled with praise ensures the presence and heartbeat of the Lord.

May my songs of worship be recorded in heaven for a divine visitation. May my journey to the mountaintop, the peak of visibility, be effortless. May every life of struggle come to an end today as I cross over to my place of inheritance. Let my mountaintop experience be permanent from this day forward, in Jesus' Name, AMEN.

Personal Prayers Journal

....

....

....

....

....

....

Day 322

*"And I will bring forth a seed out of Jacob, and out of Judah an inheritor of my mountains: **and mine elect shall inherit it, and my servants shall dwell there**" (Isaiah 65:9).*

God's elect is someone who perfectly does the will of the Father. When individuals do God's will, they are guaranteed the promise of eternal reward.

As a chosen one of God, may I inherit all the goodness that is reserved for me. May the Lord's abiding presence dwell with me every day. May I not grieve the Holy Spirit today. May I always dwell and settle in a place of abundance, in Jesus' Name, AMEN.

Personal Prayers Journal

....

....

....

....

....

....

....

Day 323

*"Notwithstanding the Lord stood with me, and strengthened me; **that by me the preaching might be fully known**, and that all the Gentiles might hear: and I was delivered out of the mouth of the lion" (2 Timothy 4:17).*

God seeks out vessels that are available for His use and will bring glory to Him. He empowers those who are willing to be a shining example to others.

May I be a vessel that is both available and deserving of being used by the Master. May my heart be filled with joy and purity as I carry out the work of the kingdom. May my life inspire others to serve Jesus Christ and not push them away. Lord, use me to lead souls to You, and may my life serve as a reflection for others to follow, starting from today, in the name of Jesus, AMEN.

Personal Prayers Journal

....

....

....

....

Day 324

*"Notwithstanding the Lord stood with me, and strengthened me; that by me the preaching might be fully known, **and that all the Gentiles might hear: and I was delivered out of the mouth of the lion**" (2 Timothy 4:17).*

We have been commissioned to spread the gospel of Christ to the nations. Our goal is to share our salvation and the light of God within us, so that it may illuminate the lives of others and guide their hearts towards Christ.

May the Lord grant me a sense of urgency to proclaim the gospel of Christ. May my words serve as a source of hope to others as I share the message. May my life be a living testimony that encourages people from all nations and tribes to accept Jesus as their Lord and Savior. I pray that the Lord grants me wisdom and a voice that cannot be disputed or resisted by anyone, starting from today, in Jesus' name.

Personal Prayers Journal

....

....

....

....

Day 325

*"Notwithstanding the Lord stood with me, and strengthened me; that by me the preaching might be fully known, and that all the Gentiles might hear: **and I was delivered out of the mouth of the lion**" (2 Timothy 4:17).*

There is no lion who can stand before the Lord, who is the Lion of the Tribe of Judah; His roar makes His enemies scatter.

———————————————

May the Lord roar and scatter every gathering of my adversaries today. May He deliver and set me free from any physical or spiritual lion that tries to devour me. Let the Lord shut the mouth of any lion that represents sickness, affliction, poverty, lack, emotional oppression, frustration, calamity, and unrest in my life, in Jesus' Name, AMEN.

Personal Prayers Journal

....

....

....

....

....

....

Day 326

*"**And the Lord shall deliver me from every evil work**, and will preserve me unto his heavenly kingdom: to whom be glory for ever and ever. Amen." (2 Timothy 4:18).*

The name of Jesus sets me above any evil work that men target against me because He is my deliverer.

May the Lord deliver me from every evil work. May His presence and power protect me from all evil plans and negative agendas of the enemy. Let the arms of the Lord cover me and shield me from any darts or arrows of the enemy today, in Jesus' Name, AMEN.

Personal Prayers Journal

....

....

....

....

....

....

....

....

Day 327

*"And the Lord shall deliver me from every evil work, **and will preserve me unto his heavenly kingdom**: to whom be glory for ever and ever. Amen." (2 Timothy 4:18).*

The promise of the Almighty God is to watch over and protect His own. No other man can preserve and protect like Him

---

Today, the Lord will arise to help me. He will send helpers to lift my hand for the completion of His kingdom mandate and assignment on earth. May I not hinder or limit the work committed into my hands. I will finish well and strong. My life will be preserved to complete all God's kingdom agenda with ease, in Jesus' Name, AMEN.

Personal Prayers Journal

....

....

....

....

....

....

Day 328

*"**For I will give you a mouth and wisdom,** which all your adversaries shall not be able to gainsay nor resist"*
(Luke 21:15).

The Lord our God is endowed with wisdom and knowledge that surpasses human understanding.

May His divine wisdom empower me as I speak solutions to lifelong problems. Let my words confound and confuse my enemies. Let the words of life that come from me be filled with power and authority, so that I may rule over nations. In Jesus' name, AMEN.

Personal Prayers Journal

....

....

....

....

....

....

....

....

....

Day 329

*"For I will give you a mouth and wisdom, **which all your adversaries shall not be able to gainsay nor resist**"*
(Luke 21:15).

There is power and authority in the word of God that terrifies and silences the devil.

May the Lord make my enemies hear a voice that fills them with despair and confusion. May my adversaries have no choice but to bow down and worship the God I serve. I will be favored and sought after. I will no longer face any resistance or rejection, but I will be accepted and lifted from glory to glory, now and always, in Jesus' Name. Amen.

Personal Prayers Journal

....

....

....

....

....

....

....

Day 330

*"**And I will bring forth a seed out of Jacob**, and out of Judah an inheritor of my mountains: and mine elect shall inherit it, and my servants shall dwell there" (Isaiah 65:9).*

The blessings of God to His beloved are not only everlasting but also extend to a thousand generations.

May my descendants be blessed and favored forever. Like Jacob, may my seed and I be rulers and kings according to an everlasting covenant. May each member of my household experience numerous testimonies, in Jesus' Name.

Personal Prayers Journal

....

....

....

....

....

....

....

....

Day 331

*"And I will bring forth a seed out of Jacob, **and out of Judah an inheritor of my mountains**: and mine elect shall inherit it, and my servants shall dwell there" (Isaiah 65:9).*

The path to the Lord's hill is dedicated to filling hearts with joyful praise and worship, in reverence and admiration of our God.

May my life be filled with joy and my heart be filled with pleasantness today. Let the words of praise burst forth from my lips as I lift up my voice. May all the blessings that will lead me to the mountaintop be released upon me today, in Jesus' name, AMEN.

Personal Prayers Journal

....

....

....

....

....

....

....

Day 332

"And I will bring forth a seed out of Jacob, and out of Judah an inheritor of my mountains: ***and mine elect shall inherit it****, and my servants shall dwell there" (Isaiah 65:9).*

God's elect refers to every believer who has a close relationship with Christ.

May my way of life leave a lasting impact and remain etched in the Father's heart for eternity. As someone chosen by God, may I always keep my reward. Let my legacy be a testimony and a monument for future generations, starting from today, in the name of Jesus, AMEN.

Personal Prayers Journal

....

....

....

....

....

....

....

....

Day 333

*"And I will bring forth a seed out of Jacob, and out of Judah an inheritor of my mountains: and mine elect shall inherit it, **and my servants shall dwell there**" (Isaiah 65:9).*

A servant's loyalty lies with the one who has paid the price for them. Therefore, my loyalty and commitment belong to Christ, who has made the ultimate sacrifice for me.

May my heart always be grateful for the sacrifice of Jesus and his precious blood. May my dwelling be in the garden of abundance. I pray that the blood of Jesus will shield and guard me against any sickness or premature death today, in the name of Jesus, AMEN.

Personal Prayers Journal

....

....

....

....

....

....

....

Day 334

"With all lowliness and gentleness, with longsuffering, bearing with one another in love" (Ephesians 4:2).

The genuine love of the Father is a powerful weapon needed to overcome the evil agenda of my tormentors.

———————————

May the God who embodies love through the ultimate sacrifice reveal Himself to me today. Let the grace to genuinely and unapologetically love others be poured out on me today, in Jesus' Name, AMEN.

Personal Prayers Journal

....

....

....

....

....

....

....

....

....

Day 335

"One God and Father of all, who is above all, and through all, and in you all" (Ephesians 4:6).

God is the true and great Father, and His love is unconditional, surpassing any comparison.

Today, may the love of God radiate all around me, filling me from within and flowing through me. May He draw me closer to Him, so that I may experience a deep intimacy and gain revelational knowledge. May I also be a witness of His good news today. In Jesus' name, AMEN.

Personal Prayers Journal

....

....

....

....

....

....

....

....

Day 336

"And I will fasten him as a nail in a sure place; and
he shall be for a glorious throne to his father's house"
(Isaiah 22:23).

God's promise to secure and keep His beloved safe is a comforting reassurance that He is with me at all times.

May the Lord bless me with His unwavering stability, replacing any insecurity. May my foundation be firmly established on the unshakeable rock of Christ. May my existence be safeguarded and anchored in Christ. May He grant me the agility of a deer's feet and strengthen my weak knees with dignity, honor, and strength today, in Jesus' Name, AMEN.

Personal Prayers Journal

....

....

....

....

....

....

....

Day 337

*"And I will fasten him as a nail in a sure place; **and he shall be for a glorious throne to his father's house**"*
(Isaiah 22:23).

A crown is traditionally bestowed upon kings and royalty. Similarly, I anticipate the celestial crown adorned with stars that is promised to all faithful followers in eternity.

May the Lord graciously adorn me with His robe of righteousness. May I be fortified and achieve success in every endeavor. May I carry my crown of grace and glory with respect and distinction. May my crown of sanctity and virtue remain steadfast, never to be displaced or traded. Let my crown grant me the authority to overcome nations and vanquish the forces of darkness today, in the name of Jesus, AMEN.

Personal Prayers Journal

....

....

....

....

....

Day 338

*"**For thou hast been a shelter for me**, and a strong tower from the enemy" (Psalms 61:3).*

When the Lord is my shelter, He surrounds me with His compassionate embrace, keeping me safe from any danger.

May the everlasting arms of the Lord safeguard and protect me. From this day forward, may the Lord keep me in His hidden haven, so that I will not stumble. May the Almighty God shield and defend me from any conspiracy against me. May He be my refuge and fortress, allowing me to remain secure and protected within His loving care and infinite arms, both now and forevermore, in Jesus' Name, AMEN.

Personal Prayers Journal

....

....

....

....

....

....

....

Day 339

*"For thou hast been a shelter for me, **and a strong tower from the enemy**" (Psalms 61:3).*

Jesus stands as the unwavering foundation in the midst of turmoil, proclaiming peace and calmness.

May the Lord be my support during times of chaos. May God guide my path each day. May He strengthen me, making me as strong as a tower and as unyielding as a rock that remains unshaken. May those who oppose me face Him as their adversary. From this day forward, may the Lord protect me at all times, surrounding me from all sides, in Jesus' name. AMEN.

Personal Prayers Journal

....

....

....

....

....

....

....

Day 340

"And the LORD turned the captivity of Job, when he prayed for his friends: also the LORD gave Job twice as much as he had before" (Job 42:10).

We are guided by a God who encompasses the true meaning of complete restoration, not only through forgiveness but also by restoring everything that has been lost.

May the Lord continuously bestow favor upon me. May God recognize and bless my offerings and efforts with abundant rewards. May I keep all the blessings I receive, both in this life and in the hereafter. For every hardship I encounter, may I be granted double the reward. As I fulfill my role as a protector for others, may I be elevated to my rightful position of honor today, in the name of Jesus, AMEN.

Personal Prayers Journal

....

....

....

....

....

....

Day 341

*"And the LORD turned the captivity of Job, when he prayed for his friends: **also the LORD gave Job twice as much as he had before**" (Job 42:10).*

God rewards and restores abundantly, granting me double blessings for every hardship I face.

———————————

May He bless my food and water, protect me from illness, disease, infirmity, plague, sorrow, oppression, spiritual attacks, and distress and spare me from the trials endured by Job. May every challenge in my life be transformed into testimonies of triumph that others will speak of, daily in Jesus' Name, AMEN.

Personal Prayers Journal

....

....

....

....

....

....

....

Day 342

*"**And that he would shew thee the secrets of wisdom, that they are double to that which is**! Know therefore that God exacteth of thee less than thine iniquity deserveth"* (Job 11:6).

The keys to divine wisdom in the lives of God's children lie in humility, a deep yearning, and an unquenchable thirst for Him.

———————————

May those around me be filled with wonder of the God I worship as He unveils the mysteries of His supreme wisdom to me this day. May the utterances from my lips draw favor and elevation my way. May God guide me to measure my words carefully, ensuring that what I say brings worth and sound advice to everyone who listens, daily, in Jesus' Name, AMEN.

Personal Prayers Journal

....

....

....

....

....

....

Day 343

*"He would show you the secrets of wisdom, for true wisdom has two sides. **Know then that God has chosen to overlook some of your iniquity.**" (Job 11:6).*

We are blessed by God, who is rich in mercy and kindness and extends grace that surpasses the scale of our transgressions.

May the Lord shower me with unmatched kindness and mercy today. May He forgive me for all my wrongdoings and cleanse me of all my sins. May He restore everything that has been diminished within me and strengthen my lineage to be sovereign and influential in His presence every day, in Jesus' Name, AMEN.

Personal Prayers Journal

....

....

....

....

....

....

Day 344

"Now the LORD blessed the latter days of Job more than his beginning" (Job 42:12).

The Lord multiplies blessings and can provide an abundance of grace and prosperity to those who trust in Him throughout their journey.

May the Lord compensate my challenges with twofold blessings. May He erase my sorrows and lead me to triumph in every aspect of life. Let the splendor of my future consistently surpass that of my past. From this day forward, may I witness comprehensive excellence in everything I undertake, in the name of Jesus. AMEN.

Personal Prayers Journal

....

....

....

....

....

....

....

Day 345

"But when that which is perfect is come, then that which is in part shall be done away" (1 Corinthians 13:10).

Achieving a fulfilling life in Christ involves developing a profound, personal connection and commitment to Him.

I pray to the Lord for His fulfillment and refinement in every area of my life, removing any hindrances or incomplete tasks that hinder my journey towards wholeness. May the time of relying solely on daily grace come to a close. May I wholeheartedly accept and encounter the multitude of blessings the Father has in store for me as I surrender myself to Him each day, in the name of Jesus, AMEN.

Personal Prayers Journal

....

....

....

....

....

....

....

Day 346

"From inside the fish Jonah prayed to the LORD his God"
(Jonah 2:1).

God is all-knowing and all-hearing, regardless of the circumstances. However, it is my responsibility to present my supplication to Him.

I pray sincerely that the Lord listens to my urgent pleas, which come from the depths of despair. I ask Him to lift me from the grip of stagnation and constraint. May I rise from the shadowed valleys of hardship and be rescued, my path set upon the heights. May His radiant light penetrate the veil of darkness that may surround me. May I emerge from the shadows and shine brightly, with the light of my spirit never to be dimmed again. I ask this in Jesus' Name, Amen.

Personal Prayers Journal

....

....

....

....

....

Day 347

"And not only so, but we glory in tribulations also: knowing that tribulation worketh patience" (Romans 5:3).

Patience is a powerful defense against the schemes of the devil, enabling the Holy Spirit to guide my reactions and responses to the challenges of life.

I pray for strength from the Lord during times of hardship and storms, so that I will not be overcome by the trials of life. May the Lord firmly establish me on solid ground as I patiently wait for His perfect timing. May my heart and soul be filled with joy as I confidently entrust all my burdens to the One who carries them, in the Name of Jesus, AMEN.

Personal Prayers Journal

....

....

....

....

....

....

....

Day 348

"And patience develops strength of character in us and helps us trust God more" (Romans. 5:4).

Patience is widely regarded as one of the most valued virtues. It is obtained through discipline.

———————————

May the Lord, in His grace, grant me the ability to wait on Him with patience. As I journey with the Lord, I pray that I do not rush ahead or lag behind. May He strengthen me both in character and in spirit, blessing my perseverance with an abundant measure of patience today, in Jesus' Name, AMEN.

Personal Prayers Journal

....

....

....

....

....

....

....

....

Day 349

"So shall my righteousness answer for me in time to come, when it shall come for my hire before thy face: every one that is not speckled and spotted among the goats, and brown among the sheep, that shall be counted stolen with me"
(Genesis 30:33).

The righteous life is rewarded by God because our God values holiness and righteousness.

_____

May the Lord protect me from the snares of sin. Let me strive each day to embody salvation by living in holiness, righteousness, and truth. May the Lord acknowledge and bless all my acts of kindness, elevating me to a position of distinction and honor, in the name of Jesus, AMEN.

Personal Prayers Journal

....

....

....

....

....

....

Day 350

*"**And hope maketh not ashamed**; because the love of God is shed abroad in our hearts by the Holy Ghost which is given unto us". (Romans 5:5).*

A loving and expectant heart attracts the Father's attention, bringing him joy as he resides in my praise.

―――――――――――

May my hope remain unshattered as I patiently wait on the Lord. May my inner thoughts and faith remain firm and unwavering, anticipating my divine visitation and blessing. May my waiting on God yield fruitful results. May my testimony unlock the book of remembrance for my benefit today, in Jesus' Name, AMEN.

Personal Prayers Journal

....

....

....

....

....

....

....

....

Day 351

*"And hope maketh not ashamed; **because the love of God is shed abroad in our hearts by the Holy Ghost which is given unto us**" (Romans 5:5).*

The gift of the Holy Spirit is freely available to everyone who has been saved and redeemed through the blood of Jesus.

———————————

May the Holy Spirit lead and guide me with His soft and gentle voice. May I experience the constant presence of His joy, peace, and goodness today. May the glory of God radiate through me, attracting people to Christ. Let the love of Jesus shine through me to everyone I interact with today, in Jesus' name, Amen.

Personal Prayers Journal

....

....

....

....

....

....

Day 352

"I take joy in doing your will, my God, for your instructions are written on my heart" (Psalms 40:8).

God grants us the gift of free will, but desires that we seek the guidance of the Holy Spirit in our daily choices.

May my commitment to following the Father's will lead to prosperity for both me and my descendants. May my relationship with God and my willingness to obey His commands grant me the privilege of His eternal presence, today and forevermore, in the name of Jesus, AMEN.

Personal Prayers Journal

....

....

....

....

....

....

....

....

....

Day 353

"There is a way that seems right to a man, but the end of it is death" (Proverbs1 4:16).

Fully surrendering to the Lord is the sole path to avoid disaster.

May I always have divine guidance as my daily compass, ensuring I stay on track and avoid the path that leads to ruin. May my journey be in alignment with divine purpose, avoiding any traps set to bring me down. Today, let me not stumble or fall into the depths of destruction. In the holy name of Jesus, AMEN.

Personal Prayers Journal

....

....

....

....

....

....

....

....

Day 354

*"**For the word of God is quick, and powerful,** and sharper than any twoedged sword, piercing even to the dividing asunder of soul and spirit, and of the joints and marrow, and is a discerner of the thoughts and intents of the heart"* (Hebrews 4:12).

The proof of life is found in breathing; the breath within me awakens and revitalizes my body, bringing it to a state of abundant life.

May God breathe new life into my body, and may any instances of barrenness or decay be revitalized by the transformative power of the precious blood of Jesus flowing through me today, in Jesus' Name, AMEN.

Personal Prayers Journal

....

....

....

....

....

....

Day 355

*"For the word of God is quick, and powerful, **and sharper than any twoedged sword, piercing even to the dividing asunder of soul and spirit, and of the joints and marrow,** and is a discerner of the thoughts and intents of the heart"* (Hebrews 4:12).

The Word of God has the power to transform the ordinary into something extraordinary and to turn speculation into reality.

May the word of life abolish barriers as immense as the Red Sea that exist between me and my destiny today. Let God's word fulfill its intended purpose in my life. May this powerful word infuse my very being with vitality and lift me above every shadow and darkness, in the name of Jesus, AMEN.

Personal Prayers Journal

....

....

....

....

....

....

Day 356

*"For the word of God is quick, and powerful, and sharper than any two-edged sword, piercing even to the dividing asunder of soul and spirit, and of the joints and marrow, **and is a discerner of the thoughts and intents of the heart"*** (Hebrews 4:12).

The Lord I serve is omniscient and omnipresent. He responds to me according to the desires of my heart.

May the contents of my heart and the words from my mouth be as pleasing as a flowing stream to the Father, who is omnipotent, omniscient, and omnipresent. Let my thoughts and actions not displease God, and may the Holy Spirit find a good and true dwelling place in my life today and always, in Jesus' name, Amen.

Personal Prayers Journal

....

....

....

....

....

Day 357

*"**And it came to pass, when Joshua was by Jericho, that he lifted up his eyes and looked**, and, behold, there stood a man over against him with his sword drawn in his hand: and Joshua went unto him, and said unto him, Art thou for us, or for our adversaries"* (Joshua 5:13).

Jericho symbolizes the barriers and periods of standstill we encounter. However, looking beyond our current challenges can lead us to our moment of triumph.

———————————

I pray that the Lord will remove any hindrance that is blocking my progress today. May this day be marked as the moment to join forces with Jesus, embracing a season of breakthrough. I ask that today, every barrier of delay, apprehension, or negativity crumbles in my path, in the powerful name of Jesus, AMEN.

Personal Prayers Journal

....

....

....

....

....

Day 358

*"And it came to pass, when Joshua was by Jericho, that he lifted up his eyes and looked, **and, behold, there stood a man over against him with his sword drawn in his hand**: and Joshua went unto him, and said unto him, Art thou for us, or for our adversaries"* (Joshua 5:13).

Being alongside a member of God's army surpasses the safety found in the midst of countless earthly military units.

May the Lord be my unwavering supporter today. Let His angels surround me with vigilance. I pray for God's fiery sword of protection to surround me, shielding me from any harm or evil this day, in the powerful name of Jesus, AMEN.

Personal Prayers Journal

....

....

....

....

....

....

....

Day 359

"And it came to pass, when Joshua was by Jericho, that he lifted up his eyes and looked, and, behold, there stood a man over against him with his sword drawn in his hand: **and Joshua went unto him, and said unto him, Art thou for us, or for our adversaries"** *(Joshua 5:13).*

Falling into God's merciful embrace is far better than being caught by adversaries.

———————————

May the Lord give me the courage to represent Him every day. Grant me the strength to resist the temptations of darkness. Today, may I witness the wonders and miracles that will transform the story of my life for the better. In Jesus' name, AMEN.

Personal Prayers Journal

....

....

....

....

....

....

Day 360

"The hand of the Lord was upon me and carried me out in the spirit of God and set me down in the midst of the valley which was full of bones" (Ezekiel 37:1).*

God's mighty hands are able to hold the entire earth, and He also carries me by His Spirit to witness His wondrous works.

May the Lord's hand be upon me for blessings. May He lift me from the shadows and place me in a position of significance. May God's Spirit carry me from the depths of darkness into His brilliant light, guiding me towards a realm of extraordinary progress today, in the name of Jesus, AMEN.

Personal Prayers Journal

....

....

....

....

....

....

....

....

Day 361

*"The hand of the Lord was upon me and carried me out in the spirit of God **and set me down in the midst of the valley which was full of bones**" (Ezekiel 37: 1).*

The wonder of the valley of the dry bones lies in the mighty hands of God, who can reverse a hopeless situation and turn it into a hopeful one.

As I step out today, may my dry bones experience be transformed into a living testimony of God's goodness through divine intervention. I will testify to God's faithfulness and mercy in my life. May my divine helpers never forget me or be late to assist me. May their timing align with God's plan to propel me forward and upward today. In Jesus' name, AMEN.

Personal Prayers Journal

....

....

....

....

....

....

Day 362

"And the same day, when the even was come, he saith unto them, Let us pass over unto the other side" (Mark 4:35).

Hearing God's voice and receiving His divine guidance brings the promise of joy and peace.

May the Lord impart vitality into my circumstances today. Let this word awaken and rejuvenate any dormant aspect of my life. May I not face the silence or absence of His divine presence and counsel today. Let my prayers and pleas receive favorable responses from the ultimate Father today, in Jesus' Name, AMEN.

Personal Prayers Journal

....

....

....

....

....

....

....

Day 363

*"And the same day, when the even was come, he saith unto them, **Let us pass over unto the other side**" (Mark 4:35).*

The ability to follow divine instructions from God results in the release of divine blessings.

———————————

As I listen attentively to the Lord's instructions and guidance today, may He bestow upon me blessings, favor, mercy, and grace beyond my expectations, requests, and imagination, in Jesus' Name, AMEN.

Personal Prayers Journal

....

....

....

....

....

....

....

....

....

....

Day 364

"Far above all principality and power and might and dominion, and every name that is named" (Ephesians 1:21).

Every demonic force and power of darkness trembles at the mention of the name of Jesus.

May I continue to walk in dominion, power, and authority over every oppression of the enemy in my life. Let the Lord arise, scatter, and frustrate every gathering against me. May there be a positive turnaround from every lament of misery to miracles today, in Jesus' mighty Name, AMEN.

Personal Prayers Journal

....

....

....

....

....

....

....

Day 365

"And the LORD had given him rest from all his enemies all around" (2 Samuel 7:1).

There is no man who can command a war when the Lord has commanded His rest.

May I enter into my seasons of rest from today. May I experience all-around rest in my going out and coming in. Let all troublemakers in my life, destiny, and enemies of progress be far away from me. May I experience and enjoy all-round peace physically, mentally, spiritually, emotionally, financially, and in terms of health from today, in Jesus' Name, AMEN.

Personal Prayers Journal

....

....

....

....

....

....

....

....

Day 366

"The LORD is far from the wicked, But He hears the prayer of the righteous" (Proverbs 15:29).

I am the righteousness of God in Christ Jesus, and because He dwells in me, every form of wickedness is uprooted.

_____

May the Lord hear and answer all my petitions to Him today. May every plan of the wicked enemies be frustrated over me, and may I receive angelic visitation with good news, favor, joy, and good tidings today, in Jesus' Name, Amen.

Personal Prayers Journal

....

....

....

....

....

....

....

....

....

Made in the USA
Columbia, SC
28 September 2024

43246388R10207